CAMBRIDGE

EMPOWER

SECOND EDITION

WORKBOOK
WITHOUT ANSWERS

T0306671

A1

STARTER

Rachel Godfrey

CONTENTS

Contents

1A I'M FROM MEXICO

1 GRAMMAR *be: I / you / we*

a Underline the correct words.

1 How *are you* / *you are*?
2 *I'm* / *I're* fine, thanks.
3 You *not are* / *aren't* in London.
4 *We're* / *We'm* from Brazil.
5 Where *am I* / *I am*?
6 **A** Are you OK?
B No, *I not am* / *I'm not*.
7 **A** Are you a student?
B Yes, *I am* / *I'm*.
8 **A** Are you from China?
B No, we *am not* / *aren't*.

b Put the words in the correct order to make sentences and questions.

1 student / a / I'm .
I'm a student.
2 teachers / aren't / We .
____
3 from / I'm / not / Turkey .
____
4 OK / Are / you ?
____
5 you / are / How ?
____
6 London / we / in / Are ?
____

2 VOCABULARY Countries

a Find seven countries in the word snake.

b Complete the sentences with the country names. Use the letters in brackets.

1 Rio de Janeiro is in ___Brazil___. (r a b i l z)
2 Rome and Bologna are in ____________. (t i l y a)
3 Tokyo is in ____________. (n a j a p)
4 Manchester and London are in ____________. (u t e h k)
5 Guadalajara is in ____________. (e c i m o x)
6 New York is in ____________. (s h u t e a)
7 Barcelona is in ____________. (n i s p a)
8 Beijing and Shanghai are in ____________. (h a n i c)

3 PRONUNCIATION
Sound and spelling: *I'm, we're*

a 01.01 Listen to the conversation. Complete the sentences.

A Hi. ____________ Hakan. What are your names?
B Hi. ____________ Carmen.
C And ____________ Camila.
A Nice to meet you. Are you from the USA?
B No, ____________ from Spain. ____________ Spanish.

1B HE'S ITALIAN

1 GRAMMAR *be: he / she / they*

a Complete the sentences with the words in the box.

is she they aren't isn't ~~are they~~ are is they are

1 Where __are they__ from?
2 **A** Are they Chinese?
B Yes, ____________.
3 **A** ____________ they Italian?
B No, ____________. They're Spanish.
4 **A** ____________ from Australia?
B Yes, she ____________.
5 **A** Is he Mexican?
B No, he ____________.

b Complete the conversations with *is, isn't, 's, are, aren't* or *'re*.

Conversation 1

A This [1] __is__ my friend Maribel.
B Where [2] ____________ she from? [3] ____________ she Brazilian?
A No, she [4] ____________. She [5] ____________ from Spain.

Conversation 2

C Who [6] ____________ Serena and Venus? [7] ____________ they volleyball players?
D No, they [8] ____________. They [9] ____________ tennis players.
C [10] ____________ they British?
D No, they [11] ____________. They [12] ____________ American.

c 01.02 Listen and check.

2 VOCABULARY Nationalities

a Complete the crossword puzzle.

→ Across

1 You're from the U.K. You're __British__.
4 She's from Japan. She's ____________.
5 He's from Australia. He's ____________.
8 We're from China. We're ____________.
9 I'm from Italy. I'm ____________.

↓ Down

1 They're from Brazil. They're ____________.
2 You're from Spain. You're ____________.
3 She's from Mexico. She's ____________.
6 We're from the USA. We're ____________.
7 He's from Turkey. He's ____________.

3 PRONUNCIATION Syllables

a 01.03 Listen to the words in the box. Complete the table.

~~British~~ Australian Chinese Italian Brazilian Turkish Japanese Spanish American Mexican

2 syllables	3 syllables	4 syllables
British		

1C EVERYDAY ENGLISH
Nice to meet you

1 USEFUL LANGUAGE
Meeting and greeting new people

a <u>Underline</u> the correct words to complete the conversations.

Conversation 1 (9 am)

DEBBIE Good [1] <u>*morning*</u> / *evening*! How are you today?
AYLA I'm not [2] *bad* / *fine*, thanks. And [3] *you* / *are you*?
DEBBIE I'm [4] *nice* / *OK*, thanks.

Conversation 2 (3 pm)

JENNY Good [5] *afternoon* / *evening*, Dean.
DEAN Hi Jenny. [6] *She* / *This* is my friend Becky.
JENNY Hi Becky. How [7] *you are* / *are you*?
BECKY I'm good, [8] *thank* / *thanks* you.
Nice [9] *to meet* / *meet* you.

b ▶01.04 Listen and check.

c Complete the conversation with the words in the box.

and ~~good~~ hello I'm is my
nice thank thanks too

CARLA [1] *Good* afternoon. [2] ______ name's Carla Watkins.
JAMES Hello. [3] ______ James Hargreaves.
CARLA [4] ______ to meet you, James.
JAMES Nice to meet you, [5] ______.
CARLA Oh, Greg! This [6] ______ James Hargreaves from Electric Blue Technology.
GREG [7] ______ James! How are you?
JAMES I'm fine, [8] ______ you. [9] ______ you?
GREG I'm good, [10] ______.

d ▶01.05 Listen and check.

2 PRONUNCIATION Sentence stress

a ▶01.06 Listen to the sentences. Which words are stressed? Tick (✓) the correct box.

1 a ☑ How <u>are</u> you?
  b ☐ <u>How</u> are you?
2 a ☐ I'm <u>fine</u>, thanks.
  b ☐ I'm fine, <u>thanks</u>.
3 a ☐ So, <u>this</u> is your office.
  b ☐ So, this is <u>your</u> office.
4 a ☐ <u>Good</u> evening!
  b ☐ Good <u>evening</u>!
5 a ☐ <u>I'm</u> Andy <u>and</u> this <u>is</u> Gaston.
  b ☐ I'm <u>Andy</u> and <u>this</u> is <u>Gaston</u>.
6 a ☐ Nice <u>to</u> meet <u>you</u>.
  b ☐ <u>Nice</u> to <u>meet</u> you.

1C SKILLS FOR WRITING
I'm Turkish

1 READING

a Read the text and tick (✓) the correct ending for the sentences.

1 Matteo is from …
  a ☑ Italy.
  b ☐ the UK.

2 He's a …
  a ☐ teacher.
  b ☐ student.

3 His teacher is …
  a ☐ British.
  b ☐ not British.

4 His friends …
  a ☐ are from Italy.
  b ☐ aren't from Italy.

5 Lia is …
  a ☐ Japanese.
  b ☐ Chinese.

6 Tamara is from …
  a ☐ Spain.
  b ☐ the USA.

Me and my friends

Hi. My name's Matteo Rossi. I'm from Naples, in Italy. I'm a student in London, in the UK. My teacher is from York, in the UK. My friends aren't from Italy or the UK. Lia is from China and Tamara is from Spain. Ana and Lucas are from Brazil.

2 WRITING SKILLS
Capital letters and full stops

a <u>Underline</u> the correct words.

Hello. 1 *my* / <u>*My*</u> name's 2 *kadim* / *Kadim.* I'm 3 *Turkish.* / *Turkish* My 4 *Friends* / *friends* are Justo and 5 *Emma.* / *Emma* 6 *They're* / *they're* very nice. Justo is from 7 *Spain* / *spain* and 8 *Emma.* / *Emma* is 9 *American.* / *American*

b Correct the sentences.

1 He's a student He's in your class.
  He's a student. He's in your class.

2 This is diana
  ____

3 My teacher is canadian.
  ____

4 their flat is in london.
  ____

5 I'm from mexico.
  ____

6 We're japanese We're from Tokyo.
  ____

3 WRITING

a Write a profile for you. Use Kadim's profile to help you.

Hi. My name's ______________________

____

____

____

____

____

____

____

____

UNIT 1
Reading and listening extension

1 READING

a Read the email and match a–d to the parts of the email 1–4.

a ☐ saying goodbye
b ☐ Mark's new job
c ☐ greeting
d ☐ people in Mark's office

b Read the email again. Are the sentences true (*T*) or false (*F*)?

1 Trevor is in Spain.
2 Mark is in Madrid.
3 Antonio is Spanish.
4 Antonio and Valeria are married.
5 Valeria is a teacher.
6 Martin is from Spain.
7 Yoko is from Japan.
8 Yoko is at home in the afternoon.

c Write an email to a friend about your new English class. Remember to say:

- where your class is
- who your teacher is and where he or she is from
- who the students are and where they are from.

Reply Forward

1 Hi Trevor,

How are you? How is Australia?

2 I'm fine. My new job in Spain is good. The office is in Madrid and it's in the centre of the city. Madrid is great!

3 I'm in an office with three people – Antonio, Martin and Yoko. Our office manager is Antonio. He isn't Spanish. He's from a small town in Mexico, but he's married to a Spanish woman. Her name's Valeria and she's a teacher in a language school. Martin is Australian. He's from Brisbane, but his home is Madrid now. Yoko is Japanese. She's from Osaka. She's in the office from 8 am to 1 pm, and she's a student at an English school in the afternoon.

4 Say hello to all my friends in Australia.

Bye for now,

Mark

2 LISTENING

a 01.07 Listen to the conversation. Tick (✓) the countries you hear.

Brazil	☐	Italy	☐
China	☐	Turkey	☐
the UK	☐	the USA	☐
Japan	☐	Spain	☐

b 01.07 Listen again and underline the correct words.

1 It is *morning* / *evening*.
2 Alice and Ryan are *at home* / *at work*.
3 *Alice* / *Ryan* is a new teacher.
4 Leeds is a city in *the UK* / *Brazil*.
5 Alice is from *Mexico* / *the USA*.
6 Ryan's class is *1A* / *1B*.
7 Daniela is a *Spanish* / *Brazilian* student.
8 Alim and Fehim are *Turkish* / *Italian*.

c Complete the conversation with your own ideas.

A Good morning.
B Hi. Are you new?
A Yes, I am. My name's ____________.
B It's nice to meet you. I'm ____________.
A Nice to meet you, too.
B Where are you from?
A ____________, in ____________.
B Really? ____________'s a nice city.

Review

1 GRAMMAR

Correct the mistakes.

1 Cara aren't Chinese. She's American.
Cara isn't Chinese. She's American.
2 **A** Where you are?
B I'm in Barcelona.
3 I not am a student. I'm a teacher.
4 **A** And who this is?
B This is Ahmet.
5 These are my friends. They Italian.
6 What your name?
7 We not Italian. We're Mexican.
8 Where Grace is from?

2 VOCABULARY

Tick (✓) the sentences that are correct. Correct the mistakes.

1 ☐ They're from UK.
They're from the UK.
2 ☐ She's Mexican.
3 ☐ He's from the Turkey.
4 ☐ She's from the USA.
5 ☐ We're Brasilian.
6 ☐ Are you Spainish?
7 ☐ I'm Japanese.
8 ☐ He's from Australia.

REVIEW YOUR PROGRESS

Look again at Review Your Progress on p. 14 of the Student's Book. How well can you do these things now?
3 = very well 2 = well 1 = not so well

I CAN ...	
say my name and country	☐
talk about people I know	☐
meet and greet new people.	☐

2A IT'S A BIG CITY

1 GRAMMAR *be: it's / it isn't*

a Underline the correct words.

1 This is Santiago. *It's / He's* a big city in Chile.
2 This is my home. *It's / They're* a small flat.
3 Evie's Australian. *It's / She's* from Perth.
4 The houses are new. *It isn't / They aren't* very big.
5 Adam is British. *He's / It's* from Birmingham.
6 **A** Is Barcelona a small city?
B No, *she isn't / it isn't*.
7 I'm from Göreme. *It's / She's* a town in Turkey.
8 **A** Are the flats in the old part of town?
B Yes, *they are / it is*.

2 GRAMMAR Possessive adjectives

a Write the correct possessive adjective. Use the pronoun in brackets to help you.

1 We're from London. ___Our___ (we) house is very old.
2 **A** What's __________ (you) name?
B I'm Celine. I'm from Paris.
3 Where's John? This is __________ (he) book.
4 **A** They're from Mexico City.
B What are __________ (they) names?
5 I'm Bruno. I'm from Italy, but __________ (I) mother is Australian.
6 This is my friend. She's from China and __________ (she) name is Jia.

3 VOCABULARY Common adjectives

a Match the **marked** words with the opposite adjectives a–g.

1 [f] It's a **big** village.
2 [ ] This book is **boring**.
3 [ ] He's a very **good** football player!
4 [ ] Why are they **happy**?
5 [ ] This vocabulary is **difficult**.
6 [ ] Is your computer **new**?
7 [ ] You're **right**.

a bad
b easy
c interesting
d old
e sad
f small
g wrong

b Look at the pictures and complete the adjectives.

1 funny

2 r____

3 d_______t

4 _oo_

5 h___y

6 b_a_____l

7 e__y

8 b____g

9 i______t__g

4 PRONUNCIATION
Sound and spelling: /h/ and /w/

a 02.01 Listen to the words in the box. Which words have the /h/ sound? Which words have the /w/ sound? Complete the table.

~~where~~ he what who his her hello when

/h/	/w/
	where

2B DO YOU HAVE A PHONE?

1 GRAMMAR Plural nouns

a Underline the correct spellings.

1 citys / cities
2 ticketes / tickets
3 watches / watchs
4 bottle of waters / bottles of water
5 knifes / knives
6 countries / countrys
7 boys / boyes
8 babies / babys
9 villages / villagees
10 keys / keyes

2 GRAMMAR *I have / you have*

a Put the words in the correct order to complete the conversation.

JESSICA Oh no!
TIMO What is it?
JESSICA My bag! It's at home!
TIMO Oh no. ¹pen / you / have / a / do ?
Do you have a pen?
JESSICA No, I don't!
TIMO Here you are. ²pens / two / I / have .
____
JESSICA Thanks.
TIMO And ³you / a / dictionary / do / have ?
____
JESSICA Yes, ⁴dictionary / have / a / I .
____
TIMO Good.
JESSICA Timo, ⁵have / you / of / bottle / do / a / water ?
____
TIMO No, I don't. Sorry. But ⁶I / apple / an / have !
____
JESSICA No thanks, Timo!

3 VOCABULARY Common objects 1

a Look at the picture and write the words.

1 a bag
2 a b__________
3 k__________
4 an u__________
5 a p__________
6 a b__________ of water

4 VOCABULARY Numbers 1

a 02.02 Listen and write the correct numbers.

1 I have eighty books.
2 __________ apples, please.
3 I have __________ bags.
4 __________ eggs, please.
5 Do you have __________ tickets?
6 __________ bottles of water, please.

5 PRONUNCIATION Sound and spelling: /s/, /z/ and /ɪz/

a 02.03 Listen to the words in the box. Is the final sound /s/, /z/ or /ɪz/? Complete the table.

~~knives~~ villages students newspapers
tickets books watches bottles houses

/s/	/z/	/ɪz/
	knives	

2C EVERYDAY ENGLISH
What's your address?

1 USEFUL LANGUAGE
Asking for and giving personal information

a Complete the questions. Use the letters in brackets.

1 What's your __address__? (s d a d r e s)
2 How do you ________ that? (l s p l e)
3 What's your ________ ________? (o n m e n u p b e r h)
4 What's your ________ ________? (s e d m d a e i l a r s)
5 What's your ________ ________? (t i n r s a f e m)

b Complete the conversation with the questions in the box.

How do you spell that?
What's your phone number?
What's your address?
~~What's your surname?~~

A [1]What's your surname?
B It's Milner.
A [2]________
B M-I-L-N-E-R.
A [3]________
B It's 39 Oak Street, Brighton.
A [4]________
B It's 07896 7421019.

c 02.04 Listen and check.

d Complete the conversation.

A What's your [1]__surname__?
B [2]________ Gibbins.
A [3]________ do you spell that?
B G-I-B-B-I-N-S.
A [4]________ your phone number?
B [5]________ 09745 833081.
A What's your email [6]________?
B [7]________ alice888@zipmail.com.

e 02.05 Listen and check.

2 PRONUNCIATION
Intonation in questions

a 02.06 Listen to the questions. Does the intonation go up (↗) or down (↘) at the end? Tick (✓) the correct box.

		↗	↘
1	How are you?	☐	✓
2	Is it a village?	☐	☐
3	What's your surname?	☐	☐
4	What's your address?	☐	☐
5	Can you spell that?	☐	☐
6	What's the spelling?	☐	☐
7	Are you from a big city?	☐	☐
8	Is this your phone?	☐	☐
9	Where are you from?	☐	☐
10	What's your email address?	☐	☐

2C SKILLS FOR WRITING

Vancouver's a great city

1 READING

a Read the information. Complete the form with the words in the box.

Simmons British Office
Gem ~~Eve~~ 745 9178

MONTY'S BOOK COMPANY

OUR PEOPLE

Hi. My name's Eve Simmons. I'm from the UK but I live here in Canada. Vancouver's a great city and I'm very happy here! My office is in the Gem Building in White Street. I'm in Room 745 with Kadim Baydar and Sandro Alessi. Our office phone number is 8969. My email address is evesim9178@travelmail.com.

First name:	1 Eve
Surname:	2 ______
Nationality:	3 ______
Home address:	331 Ash Street, Apartment 2, Vancouver
Phone number:	(604) 555-1478
Office address:	Room 4 ______, The 5 ______ Building, White Street, Vancouver
6 ______ **phone number:**	8969
Email address:	evesim 7 ______@travelmail.com

2 WRITING SKILLS
The alphabet and spelling

a Underline the letter with the different sound.

1 A J K <u>R</u>
2 B C D F
3 M N G S
4 O Q U W
5 I X Y

b Correct the spellings.

1 bottel bottle
2 spel ______
3 eesy ______
4 fone ______
5 addres ______
6 villige ______
7 hapy ______
8 nashionality ______
9 offis ______
10 emale ______

3 WRITING

a Complete the form with information about you.

First name:	______
Surname:	______
Nationality:	______
Home address:	______ ______
Phone number:	______
Email address:	______

UNIT 2
Reading and listening extension

1 READING

a Read the text. Tick (✓) the correct summary 1–4.

1 ☐ Maria and Rafael are married. They are managers in Bilbao. They have a house in a village near Bilbao.
2 ☐ Maria and Rafael are married. They have a house in Bilbao. Rafael is a manager in a small town near Bilbao.
3 ☐ Maria and Rafael have a house in Bilbao. They are receptionists in a big office in Bilbao.
4 ☐ Rafael is a receptionist in Bilbao. He is married to Maria. They have a house in a town near Bilbao.

b Read the text again. Tick (✓) the correct answer.

1 Is Bilbao a small town?
a ☐ Yes, it is.
b ☑ No, it isn't.

2 Is Bilbao rainy?
a ☐ Yes, it is.
b ☐ No, it isn't.

3 Is it a boring place?
a ☐ Yes, it is.
b ☐ No, it isn't.

4 Is Rafael's office near an airport?
a ☐ Yes, it is.
b ☐ No, it isn't.

5 Is Lekeitio a big town?
a ☐ Yes, it is.
b ☐ No, it isn't.

6 Is Maria and Rafael's house new?
a ☐ Yes, it is.
b ☐ No, it isn't.

7 Is their house near a supermarket?
a ☐ Yes, it is.
b ☐ No, it isn't.

8 Is Rafael happy?
a ☐ Yes, he is.
b ☐ No, he isn't.

ABOUT

My name is Rafael Reyes and I work in Bilbao in Spain. Bilbao is a big city with 345,000 people. It's rainy here and the city has an interesting history. I'm a receptionist in an office in the centre of Bilbao. My office is in a nice part of the city. It's near a big park.

My home isn't in Bilbao. It's in Lekeitio. Lekeitio is a small town near Bilbao with about 7,000 people. It's a nice town with a park, two supermarkets and a hotel. I'm married to Maria and we have two children.

Our house is in the centre of Lekeitio. It's a small house and it's new. It isn't near the park, but it is near one of the supermarkets. I'm very happy here. I have a lot of friends in Lekeitio and in Bilbao, and my job isn't boring!

c Write about your home. Think about these questions:

- Where is your home?
- Is your home big or small? Is it old or new?
- Is your home in a small town, a city or a village?
- Is your town, city or village interesting or boring?
- What is near your home?

2 LISTENING

a 02.07 Listen. Complete the sentences with the words in the box.

one desk two desks three desks

1 Speaker 1, Darren, has ____________.
2 Speaker 2, Paula, has ____________.
3 Speaker 3, Jamie, has ____________.

b 02.07 Listen again. Match pictures a–c to speakers 1–3.

1 ☐ Darren 2 ☐ Paula 3 ☐ Jamie

c 02.07 Listen again. What does each person have on his or her desk? Complete the table with the words in the box.

apple glass of water keys bag knife
laptop newspaper ~~phone~~ umbrella

Darren	Paula	Jamie
phone		

d Write about your desk. Use the Audioscript on p. 82 to help you. Think about these questions:

- Where is your desk?
- Is your desk old or new?
- Is your desk big or small?
- What is on your desk?
- What isn't on your desk?

Review

1 GRAMMAR

Correct the mistakes.

1 Is this you computer?
Is this your computer?
2 I have three watch.
3 They're a beautiful village.
4 Beijing is a big cities.
5 This is Kira and Paul and this is they're house.
6 My flat is in an old part of town. They're very small.
7 Where's Anna? This is she's bag.
8 Where are the knifes?

2 VOCABULARY

Correct the spelling.

1 eigt tickets
eight tickets
2 smal bottles of water
3 thirten flats
4 an intresting city
5 twelv phones
6 beatiful houses
7 an old umbrela
8 funy books

REVIEW YOUR PROGRESS

Look again at Review Your Progress on p. 22 of the Student's Book. How well can you do these things now?
3 = very well 2 = well 1 = not so well

I CAN ...	
talk about my home town	☐
talk about possessions and common objects	☐
ask for and give personal information.	☐

3A DO YOU LIKE FISH?

1 GRAMMAR
Present simple: *I / you / we / they*

a Underline the correct words.

1 We *fruit eat* / *eat fruit* every day.
2 *Do you eat* / *You eat* bread?
3 They *no eat* / *don't eat* eggs.
4 **A** Do you like vegetables?
  B No, *don't* / *I don't*.
5 *Like you* / *Do you like* fish?
6 **A** Do you like meat?
  B No, we *don't like* / *don't*.
7 I *don't like* / *not like* rice.
8 **A** Do you like fruit?
  B Yes, I *do* / *like*.

b 03.01 Listen and check.

c Complete the conversation with the words in the box.

do like don't you eat do you ~~like meat~~ don't eat

DUNCAN Mmm! I [1] like meat ! I eat meat every day!
RAJIT Really? I [2]__________ meat.
DUNCAN Oh, you don't eat meat. Do [3]__________ fish?
RAJIT No, I [4]__________.
DUNCAN [5]__________ eat eggs?
RAJIT Yes, I [6]__________. I [7]__________ eggs.

d 03.02 Listen and check.

2 VOCABULARY Food 1

a Write the words under the pictures.

meat vegetables ~~fish~~ milk tea cola
bread rice coffee juice eggs fruit

1 fish

2 __________

3 __________

4 __________

5 __________

6 __________

7 __________

8 __________

9 __________

10 __________

11 __________

12 __________

b Complete the crossword puzzle.

→ Across
2 C__________ is a drink. It's from Brazil, Colombia and other countries.
6 V__________ are food. They're good for you.
7 W__________ is a drink. It's good for you.
10 E__________ are food from chickens.
11 C__________ is a drink. It isn't very good for you!

↓ Down
1 Lots of people eat bread every day.
3 F__________ juice is a drink.
4 F__________ is food. It's an animal in the sea.
5 M__________ is food from animals.
8 R__________ is food. It's from China, India and other countries.
9 Lots of people drink t__________ every day.

3 PRONUNCIATION Sound and spelling: /iː/, /ɪ/ and /aɪ/

a 03.03 Listen to the words in the box. What sound do the **marked** letters have? Complete the table.

~~my~~ t**ea** th**i**s r**i**ce m**i**lk **i**s
I w**e** l**i**ke **I**taly m**ea**t k**ey**

/iː/ (e.g., *be*)	/ɪ/ (e.g., *it*)	/aɪ/ (e.g., *by*)
		my

3B I USUALLY HAVE DINNER EARLY

1 GRAMMAR Adverbs of frequency

a Underline the correct words.

1 We <u>*sometimes have*</u> / *have sometimes* eggs for breakfast.
2 I *eat never* / *never eat* biscuits at work.
3 You *have usually* / *usually have* a sandwich for lunch.
4 They *have always* / *always have* cake at the weekend.
5 I *sometimes eat* / *eat sometimes* an apple at lunchtime.
6 I *have never* / *never have* dinner at 7:00.

b Look at the table and complete the sentences. Use *always*, *usually*, *sometimes* or *never* and the present simple of the verbs in brackets.

1 I ___never eat___ fish. (eat)
2 I ________ lunch in a café. (eat)
3 I ________ rice for lunch. (eat)
4 I ________ lunch at work. (have)
5 I ________ cereal for breakfast. (have)
6 I ________ dinner at home. (have)

Food and me	
eat fish	x
eat lunch in a café	every day
eat rice for lunch	on Wednesdays and Saturdays
have lunch at work	x
have cereal for breakfast	on Mondays, Tuesdays, Wednesdays, Thursdays and Fridays
have dinner at home	every day

2 VOCABULARY Food 2

a Underline the correct words to complete the conversations.

1 **A** What fruit do you like?
B Apples and *sandwiches* / *potatoes* / <u>*bananas*</u>.
2 **A** Would you like *a biscuit* / *butter* / *a pizza* with your coffee?
B No thanks.
3 **A** A *sandwich* / *pizza* / *tomato* is a vegetable.
B No, it isn't. It's a fruit!
4 **A** We have bread, butter and eggs.
B Good! *An egg sandwich* / *A cake* / *An apple* for me, please.
5 **A** A cheese and tomato *apple* / *pizza* / *ice cream*, please.
B Certainly.
6 **A** Is this fruit juice?
B Yes, it's *cake* / *orange* / *cheese* juice.

b 03.04 Listen and check.

3 VOCABULARY Time

a Look at the clocks and complete the times. Use the words in the box.

eleven half ~~o'clock~~ past quarter (x2) ten to

1 eight ___o'clock___

5 half past ________

2 quarter ________ seven

6 ________ to one

3 ________ o'clock

7 quarter ________ six

4 ________ past one

8 ________ past one

b 03.05 Listen and check.

4 PRONUNCIATION Sound and spelling: /ɑː/ and /ɔː/

a 03.06 Listen to the words in the box. What sound do the **marked** letters have? Complete the table.

~~morning~~ afternoon half past always four water class banana small

/ɑː/ (e.g., *car*)	/ɔː/ (e.g., *your*)
	morning

3C EVERYDAY ENGLISH
I'd like a cup of tea, please

1 USEFUL LANGUAGE
Ordering and paying in a café

a Complete the expressions with the words in the box.

water sandwich ~~coffee~~ are course cake

1 a cup of ___*coffee*___
2 a piece of ________
3 here you ________
4 a glass of ________
5 a cheese ________
6 of ________

b Complete the conversation with the sentences in the box.

No, thanks.
Can I have a cup of coffee, please?
OK. Thank you very much.
~~Hello. I'd like a piece of fruit cake, please.~~

WAITRESS Good morning.
NANCY 1 *Hello. I'd like a piece of fruit cake, please.*
WAITRESS Certainly. And to drink?
NANCY 2 ________
WAITRESS Of course. With milk?
NANCY 3 ________
WAITRESS Here you are. That's £6.50, please.
NANCY 4 ________
WAITRESS Thank you.

c 03.07 Listen and check.

d Underline the correct words to complete the conversation.

WAITER Good afternoon.
SAM Hello. 1 *I have / I'd like* a cup of tea, please.
WAITER Sure. And to 2 *eat / drink*?
SAM 3 *I'd like / I like* a cheese sandwich, please.
WAITER With tomato?
SAM No, thanks. And 4 *I'd / can I* have some chocolate cake and a glass 5 *water / of water* too, please?
WAITER Of course! That's £11, please.
SAM OK. Here 6 *you are / are you.*
WAITER Thank you.

e 03.08 Listen and check.

2 PRONUNCIATION
Sentence stress

a 03.09 Listen to the phrases. Which words are stressed? Tick (✓) the correct box.

1 a [ ] a slice of pizza
  b [✓] a slice of pizza
2 a [ ] a cup of coffee
  b [ ] a cup of coffee
3 a [ ] a glass of water
  b [ ] a glass of water
4 a [ ] a piece of cheese
  b [ ] a piece of cheese
5 a [ ] a glass of fruit juice
  b [ ] a glass of fruit juice
6 a [ ] a cup of tea
  b [ ] a cup of tea
7 a [ ] a glass of milk
  b [ ] a glass of milk
8 a [ ] a piece of chocolate cake
  b [ ] a piece of chocolate cake

3C SKILLS FOR WRITING
I'm in a café

1 READING

a Read the text messages. Are the sentences true (*T*) or false (*F*)?

1 Tony's with a friend from Spain.
2 Javier's funny.
3 Evie's at work.
4 Felipe and Evie are students.
5 Omar likes his work.
6 Renata's at work.

Tony: Hi Lisa. I'm in a café with Javier. He's my new friend. He's Spanish. He's very funny. Talk soon!

Evie: Hi Misha. I'm in a restaurant with Felipe. He's a student in my class. We like our new teacher very much. She's from Sydney. See you later!

Omar: Hi Renata. I'm at work. It's boring! Where are you? Why aren't you here? Talk to you soon.

2 WRITING SKILLS Contractions

a Write the full form of the contractions.

1 I'm ___I am___
2 She isn't ______
3 He's ______
4 We don't ______
5 They aren't ______
6 It's ______

b Complete the text messages with the words in brackets. Use contractions.

1 Hi Emre. ___I'm___ (I am) in a café with Julio and Marta. ______ (They are) really nice! See you later!
2 Hi Frida. ______ (We are) at the restaurant. ______ (You are not) here! Where are you?
3 Hi Danny. I ______ (do not) like work! It's boring.
4 Hi Mel. ______ (We are) in Rome. ______ (It is) a beautiful city! Talk later!
5 Hi Greg. ______ (I am) at work with Robert. ______ (He is not) very happy.
6 Hi Matt. ______ (I am not) happy today. My teacher is boring.

3 WRITING

a Write a text message to a friend. Think about these questions:

- Where are you?
- Are you at work?
- Who are you with?

UNIT 3
Reading and listening extension

1 READING

a Read about meals in Italy. Underline the correct words to complete the sentences.

1 In Italy, people <u>*eat*</u> / *don't eat* a lot of fruit and vegetables.
2 Italians drink a lot of *tea* / *coffee.*
3 They *like* / *don't like* meat and fish.
4 They usually have *three* / *four* meals every day.
5 Italian people *have* / *don't have* pasta every day.
6 For a lot of people, the big meal of the day is in the *afternoon* / *evening.*

b Read the text again. Are the sentences true (*T*) or false (*F*)?

1 Breakfast is at 9:00.
2 Maria and her family have coffee and cereal for breakfast.
3 On work days, Maria and her friends have lunch in the office.
4 At weekends, Maria has lunch with her family.
5 A *panino* is a pizza.
6 Dinner is at 8:30.
7 They sometimes have pasta for dinner.
8 They often have cake in the morning.

c Write about the meals you have every day. Think about these questions:

- How many meals do you have?
- What time do you have your meals?
- What do you usually have for breakfast, lunch and dinner?

MEALS IN ITALY

My name is Maria and I'm Italian. In Italy, people eat different kinds of food. We like pasta and pizza, but we don't eat them every day. We like a lot of different meat and fish. And we eat a lot of fruit and vegetables.

In my family, we have three meals a day. Breakfast is at eight o'clock. We eat *fette biscottate*, a type of breakfast bread, and have coffee with milk. Italian people usually drink a lot of coffee!

On work days, my lunch is always at one o'clock. I never have lunch in my office. I usually have a *panino* (that's a sandwich) or a slice of pizza with my friends in a café near the office. At the weekend, I have lunch at home with my family.

Dinner is the big meal of the day for a lot of Italians. In my family, we always have dinner at half past eight. We have rice or pasta, then fish with vegetables. We don't eat a lot of meat. After dinner, we usually have fruit and coffee, but at the weekend we sometimes have cake.

2 LISTENING

a 03.10 Listen to the conversation. Tick (✓) the food and drink words you hear.

cheese	☑	banana	☐
meat	☐	ice cream	☐
egg	☐	tea	☐
fish	☐	fruit juice	☐
chocolate	☐	water	☐

b 03.10 Listen again. Tick (✓) who says the sentences.

	John	Anna
1 I never eat cheese.	✓	
2 Do you like eggs?		
3 I like eggs.		
4 I eat a lot of tomatoes.		
5 I don't eat a lot of chocolate.		
6 I usually drink tea.		
7 I don't like hot drinks.		
8 I always have orange juice for breakfast.		

c Write about food and drinks you like and don't like. Use these expressions:

- I eat a lot of …
- I don't drink a lot of …
- I never eat …
- I always drink …

Review

1 GRAMMAR

Tick (✓) the sentences that are correct. Correct the mistakes.

1 ☑ Do you like eggs?
2 ☐ I never eat cake.
3 ☐ We have sometimes pizza.
4 ☐ They don't like ice cream.
5 ☐ I like fruit.
6 ☐ I not like cheese.
7 ☐ You like meat?
8 ☐ They eat usually pizza for lunch.

2 VOCABULARY

Tick (✓) the sentences that are correct. Correct the mistakes.

1 ☐ I like vegtables.
I like vegetables.
2 ☐ We have lunch at 12:45 pm.
3 ☐ We eat rise for lunch every day.
4 ☐ Do you have an apple?
5 ☐ I never eat biscits.
6 ☐ We have a breakfast at 7:30 am.
7 ☐ I don't like cake.
8 ☐ That sanwich is really big!

REVIEW YOUR PROGRESS

Look again at Review Your Progress on p. 30 of the Student's Book. How well can you do these things now?
3 = very well 2 = well 1 = not so well

I CAN …	
say what I eat and drink	☐
talk about food and meals	☐
order and pay in a café.	☐

4A WHAT DO YOU STUDY?

1 GRAMMAR
Present simple: *Wh-* questions

a Put the words in the correct order to make questions.

1 live / where / do / you ?
<u>*Where do you live?*</u>
2 's / flat / your / where ?
____
3 lunch / eat / what / for / you / do ?
____
4 are / names / their / what ?
____
5 do / study / where / you ?
____
6 start / when / she / work / does ?
____

b <u>Underline</u> the correct words.

1 What time *is* / *are* / <u>*do*</u> you go to the gym?
2 What languages *is* / *are* / *do* you speak?
3 What *is* / *are* / *do* the time?
4 When *is* / *are* / *do* you meet your friends?
5 Where *is* / *are* / *do* you from?
6 Where *is* / *are* / *do* the university?
7 When *is* / *are* / *do* you at home?
8 What *is* / *are* / *do* you study?

2 VOCABULARY Common verbs

a Tick (✓) the correct words to complete the sentences.

1 You ______________ Spanish.
a ☐ live b ☑ speak c ☐ meet
2 We ______________ Japanese.
a ☐ meet b ☐ study c ☐ work
3 I ______________ my friends every day.
a ☐ meet b ☐ go c ☐ work
4 We ______________ football.
a ☐ go b ☐ play c ☐ speak
5 I ______________ at an English language school.
a ☐ go b ☐ live c ☐ teach
6 We ______________ to the gym every day.
a ☐ go b ☐ study c ☐ teach

b Complete the crossword puzzle.

→ Across
2 They ______________ to school every day.
4 I ______________ English, Spanish and Turkish.
5 I ______________ young children in a small school.
6 We ______________ tennis every day.

↓ Down
1 I <u>*work*</u> in a factory.
3 I ______________ my friends after school.
4 We ______________ English at a language school.
7 You ______________ in a big house.

3 PRONUNCIATION Stressed words

a 04.01 Listen to the sentences and <u>underline</u> the stressed words.

1 <u>Where</u> do you <u>live</u>?
2 Do you speak French?
3 Do you work in a factory?
4 What do you study?
5 Do you go to the gym?
6 When do you have lunch?

4B SHE HAS A SISTER AND A BROTHER

1 GRAMMAR
Present simple: *he / she / it* positive

a Underline the correct words.

1 Pablo *haves* / *has* an international family.
2 My dad *teachs* / *teaches* at the university.
3 Julie *lives* / *livs* in a big house.
4 Sandro *works* / *workes* in an office.
5 My brother *studys* / *studies* maths.
6 Camila *plays* / *playes* the guitar.
7 Ryan *speakes* / *speaks* Chinese.
8 My mum *goes* / *gos* to the gym every day.

b Complete the sentences with the correct form of the verbs in brackets.

1 Dean ___likes___ tennis and football. (like)
2 My sister __________ to the cinema every weekend. (go)
3 Jack __________ Italian at university. (study)
4 Mandy __________ a sister and two brothers. (have)
5 My brother __________ cola every day. (drink)
6 My mum __________ young children. (teach)
7 Enrique __________ at home. (work)
8 My friend Sonya __________ in Berlin. (live)

2 VOCABULARY Numbers 2

a Write the numbers in words.

51 ___fifty-one___
27 __________
45 __________
89 __________
34 __________
98 __________
66 __________
100 __________
72 __________

3 VOCABULARY Family and people

a Look at the family tree. Complete the sentences with the words in the box.

brother	daughter	father	~~husband~~
mother	parents	sister	son	wife

1 Michael is Jane's ___husband___.
2 Michael is Natalie's __________.
3 Jane is Oliver's __________.
4 Ron and Mary are Laura's __________.
5 Oliver is Natalie's __________.
6 Diana is Ron's __________.
7 Oliver is Michael's __________.
8 Natalie is James's __________.
9 Laura is Diana's __________.

4 PRONUNCIATION
Sound and spelling: /ð/

a 04.02 Listen and tick (✓) the words that have the /ð/ sound.

1 she ☐
2 that ☐
3 right ☐
4 father ☐
5 mother ☐
6 three ☐
7 they ☐
8 the ☐
9 eight ☐
10 brother ☐

4C EVERYDAY ENGLISH
This is me with my father

1 USEFUL LANGUAGE
Asking and talking about photos

a Underline the correct words to complete the conversation.

CATH [1]*Can I see* / *Do you have* photos of your home?
AMY Yes, [2]*I do* / *do*.
CATH [3]*Can I see* / *This is* them?
AMY Sure. [4]*This is* / *This* my flat.
CATH [5]*Who does* / *Who's* this?
AMY My brother Harry.
CATH [6]*Great* / *Is great* photo!
AMY Thanks. Here's another picture of my flat.
CATH [7]*It* / *It's* really nice.

b 04.03 Listen and check.

c Put the conversation in the correct order.

☐ **JENNY** Nice picture!
☐ **JENNY** They're lovely. Thank you.
1 **JENNY** Do you have photos of your family?
☐ **JENNY** Can I see them?
☐ **SEAN** And this is me with my mum and my sister.
☐ **SEAN** Sure. This is my dad and my brother.
☐ **SEAN** Yes, I do.

d 04.04 Listen and check.

2 PRONUNCIATION
Sound and spelling: /tʃ/ and /dʒ/

a 04.05 Listen to the words in the box. What sound do the **marked** letters have? Complete the table.

~~oran**ge**~~ ques**ti**on **ch**eap pa**g**e **ch**ild **J**apan ve**g**etable mana**g**er pic**t**ure wa**tch**

/tʃ/ (e.g., *lun**ch***)	/dʒ/ (e.g., *lar**ge***)
	orange

4C SKILLS FOR WRITING
They're a happy family

1 READING

a Read about the photo. Underline the correct answers.

1 Hugo is *six* / *thirty-six*.
2 Luis and Hugo live in a *small* / *big* house.
3 They live in *Spain* / *Brazil*.
4 Luis works with *children* / *computers*.
5 Luis *is* / *isn't* married.
6 Juliana is a university *teacher* / *student*.
7 She *lives in* / *is from* Brazil.
8 Juliana, Luis and Hugo *are* / *aren't* happy.

2 WRITING SKILLS Word order

a Tick (✓) the correct sentences.

1 a [✓] We don't work.
  b [ ] We work don't.
2 a [ ] We have a big meal in the evening.
  b [ ] We have in the evening a big meal.
3 a [ ] They don't have a pencil in their bag.
  b [ ] They don't have in their bag a pencil.
4 a [ ] We play at school football.
  b [ ] We play football at school.
5 a [ ] I like in my coffee sugar.
  b [ ] I like sugar in my coffee.
6 a [ ] She doesn't in London work.
  b [ ] She doesn't work in London.

b Put the words in the correct order to make sentences.

1 his daughters / this / is / my friend / with .
This is my friend with his daughters.
2 Milan / live / they / in .
______
3 here / I / live / don't .
______
4 Ruben and Cara / these / children / are / my .
______
5 a / Mexico / have / flat / small / I / City / in .
______
6 English / at / sister / my / university / studies .
______

3 WRITING

a Write a caption for a favourite photo of you with your friends or family. Remember to give information about:

- who the people are
- where they are
- their jobs or studies.

______
______
______
______

UNIT 4
Reading and listening extension

1 READING

a Read the email and match the people 1–6 to the places a–f.

1	[e] Daniel	a	Melbourne
2	[ ] Zeynep	b	Kyoto
3	[ ] Elizabetta	c	Istanbul
4	[ ] Greg and Claire	d	San Francisco
5	[ ] Jon	e	Mexico City
6	[ ] Tom	f	Washington

b Read the email again. Complete the family tree with the names in the box.

Jeff Keiko Rei ~~Elizabetta~~
Claire Daniel Greg Tom

Hi Zeynep,

Thanks for your email. I love the photos of your family. You have a big family! My family is small. Here's a photo of us on holiday.

I'm with my husband, Greg, our daughter, Linda, and our son, Jeff. My parents, Tom and Elizabetta, are in the photo, too. My dad is American. He's from San Francisco, but my mother comes from Melbourne in Australia. Greg and I live in Washington with our children. Greg works in an office and I'm a teacher (as you know). Greg's parents live in Washington, too, so we see them one or two days a week, but my mum and dad are in California. We usually see them during the summer.

I have two brothers, Daniel and Jon. They're not in the photo. Daniel is an English teacher in Mexico City and Jon lives in Kyoto, in Japan. Jon's wife, Keiko, is Japanese and they have a daughter. Her name's Rei. We sometimes see them during the summer. Rei is five and she speaks Japanese and English very well.

Write soon and tell me more about your life in Istanbul.

Claire

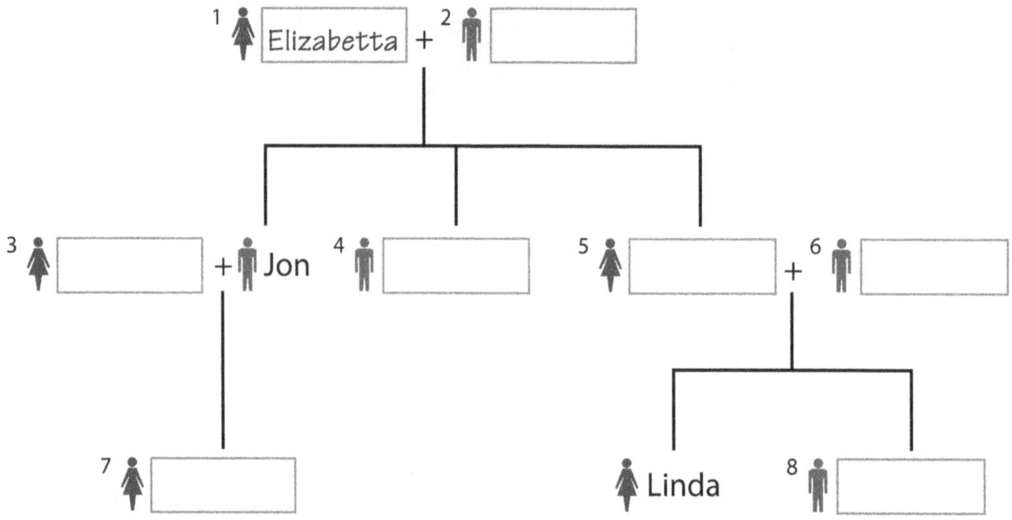

c Draw your family tree and write about the people in your family. Write about:

- their names and ages
- their jobs or studies
- where they live.

Review

1 GRAMMAR

Correct the mistakes.

1 Where you study?
Where do you study?
2 He work in Barcelona.
3 She haves two brothers.
4 What your name is?
5 Her husband gos to work in the evening.
6 My sister studys German.
7 Where live you?
8 Where you from?

2 VOCABULARY

Tick (✓) the sentences that are correct. Correct the mistakes.

1 ☑ I teach children.
2 ☐ Our English class has six woman and two men.
3 ☐ I speak Turkish.
4 ☐ My sister is twenty and five years old.
5 ☐ I study at university.
6 ☐ Their son is thirty-three and their daugter is thirty-five.
7 ☐ His mother is hundred years old.
8 ☐ I meet interesting peoples at work.

2 LISTENING

a 04.06 Listen to the conversation. Put the subjects in the order you hear them.

☐ a holiday
☐ language lessons
☐ working at a university
☐ parents
1 studying at a university

b 04.06 Listen again and underline the correct words.

1 *Bob* / *Kerry* has a job.
2 *Bob* / *Kerry* lives in London.
3 *Bob* / *Kerry* studies at university.
4 *Bob* / *Kerry* works in Hong Kong.
5 *Bob* / *Kerry* lives in a house with other students.
6 *Bob* / *Kerry* has language classes.
7 *Bob* / *Kerry* is on holiday.
8 *Bob's* / *Kerry's* parents live in France.

c Complete the conversation with your own ideas.

A Hi, ____________!
B Hello, ________. How are you?
A I'm fine, thanks. I'm a student at ____________ University now.
B Really? What subject do you ____________?
A ____________. Where do you ____________ now?
B I live in ____________ and I work ____________ an office.
A That's good.
B How ____________ your parents?
A They're fine. They live in ____________ now.
B Really? That's great.

REVIEW YOUR PROGRESS

Look again at Review Your Progress on p. 38 of the Student's Book. How well can you do these things now?
3 = very well 2 = well 1 = not so well

I CAN ...	
talk about my life and ask about others	☐
talk about my family	☐
ask and talk about photos.	☐

5A THERE ARE A FEW SHOPS

1 GRAMMAR
there is / there are: positive

a Put the words in the correct order to make sentences.

1 here / there / 's / school / one .
There's one school here.
2 teachers / two / there / are .
______
3 cars / are / few / a / there .
______
4 a / there / 's / small / museum .
______
5 are / families / ten / there .
______
6 there / old / an / 's / hospital .
______

b 05.01 Listen and check.

c Complete the sentences with *there's* or *there are*.

1 There are a lot of people.
2 ______ a good café in the old town.
3 ______ an interesting shop on this street.
4 ______ about 50 families.
5 ______ a few new houses and flats.
6 ______ a very small school.
7 ______ 72 big houses.
8 ______ one bank.

2 PRONUNCIATION
Sound and spelling: /uː/ and /ʌ/

a 05.02 Listen to the words in the box. What sound do the **marked** letters have? Complete the table.

f**ew** b**u**tter s**o**metimes s**u**permarket sch**oo**l st**u**dy
b**eau**tiful f**oo**d l**o**ve wh**o** f**u**nny m**o**ther

/uː/ (e.g., *you*)	/ʌ/ (e.g., *cup*)
few	

3 VOCABULARY Places in a town

a Write the words under the pictures.

park hospital ~~shop~~ hotel beach café cinema
school bank museum restaurant swimming pool

1 shop

2 ______

3 ______

4 ______

5 ______

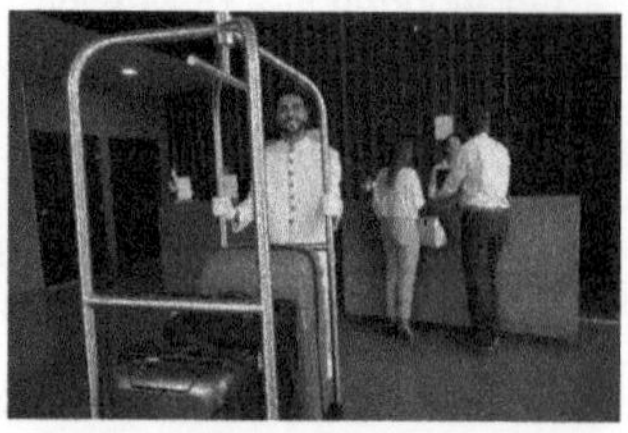
6 ______

7 ______

8 ______

9 ______

10 ______

11 ______

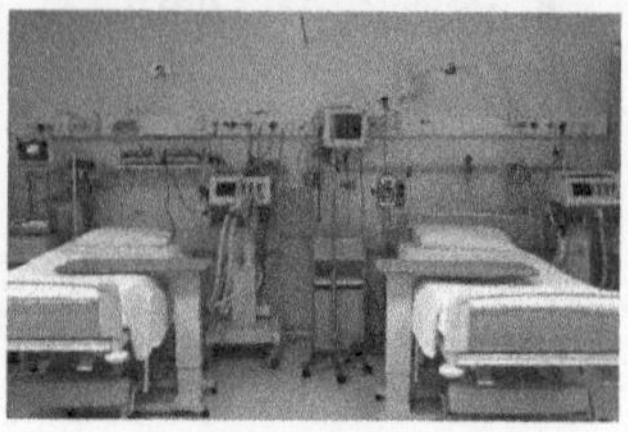
12 ______

5B IS THERE A HOSTEL IN YOUR TOWN?

1 GRAMMAR *there is / there are*: negative and questions

a Tick (✓) the correct words to complete the sentences.

1 There isn't ________ in the room.
a ☑ a TV b ☐ two TVs

2 Are there any good ________ in this town?
a ☐ restaurant b ☐ restaurants

3 There aren't ________ on the first floor.
a ☐ a big room b ☐ any big rooms

4 There aren't any ________ here.
a ☐ car park b ☐ car parks

5 Is there ________ near here?
a ☐ a café b ☐ any cafés

6 Is there ________ near the station?
a ☐ a bank b ☐ banks

b Underline the correct words to complete the conversations.

Conversation 1

A [1]*There is* / *<u>Is there</u>* a bath in the room?
B No, there [2]*isn't* / *aren't*. But there [3]*are* / *is* a shower.

Conversation 2

A There [4]*aren't any* / *isn't a* hotels in this town.
B Oh.
A [5]*There aren't any* / *There's a* hostel on King Street. It's very good.
B OK. Thanks.

Conversation 3

B Is there [6]*any* / *a* car park for this hotel?
A Yes, [7]*there is* / *is there*.
B [8]*Are there any* / *Is there an* empty rooms on the ground floor?
A No, there [9]*aren't* / *isn't*. Sorry. There [10]*are* / *isn't* a lot of empty rooms on the top floor.
B Oh. No thanks.

c 05.03 Listen and check.

2 PRONUNCIATION Sound and spelling: /ʃ/

a 05.04 Listen and tick (✓) the words that have the /ʃ/ sound.

1 ☐ bath
2 ☐ shower
3 ☐ China
4 ☐ Turkish
5 ☐ she
6 ☐ sure
7 ☐ six
8 ☐ finish
9 ☐ museum
10 ☐ shop
11 ☐ station
12 ☐ cinema

3 VOCABULARY Hotels

a Complete the sentences. Use the letters in brackets.

1 There's a big ___bath___, but there isn't any hot water. (a h b t)
2 It's very cold. Can I have a ________ for my bed, please? (n e k l a b t)
3 There's free ________-________ here, but I don't have my tablet with me. (f i i w)
4 The ________'s very good and there's lots of hot water. (o r w s h e)
5 There's a big ________ for meetings on the second floor. (o m o r)
6 Can I have a ________, please? I want to go to the swimming pool. (o w e l t)
7 **A** Where's the car?
B It's in the ________ ________. (p r a c k r a)
8 There's one small ________ on the bed. (w o l p l i)

b Complete the crossword puzzle.

→ Across

1 I often sit in a ___bath___ of hot water to relax.
3 There are a lot of cars in the car ________.
4 **A** Jason's at the swimming pool.
B Does he have his ________?
A Oh no! It's on his bed.
6 **A** Can I have a ________?
B Sorry, there isn't any hot water.

↓ Down

1 **A** I'm cold.
B Put a ________ on the bed.
2 Do you like watching films on ________ or at the cinema?
3 **A** There are three big ________ on my bed.
B Give me one for my head.
5 **A** There isn't any ________-________.
B Oh, that's OK. I don't need to use the Internet.
7 We need two ________ at the hotel. One for my parents and one for my brother and me.

5C EVERYDAY ENGLISH
Is there a supermarket near here?

1 USEFUL LANGUAGE
Asking and saying where places are

a Complete the sentences and questions with the words in the box.

it's near ~~where's~~ there there's

1 __Where's__ the hospital?
2 Is ________ a park near here?
3 Are there any restaurants ________ here?
4 ________ one in this street.
5 ________ in the next street.

b Complete the conversation with the sentences in the box.

OK. And is there a museum near here?
Oh yes! Great! Thanks for your help.
~~Excuse me, can you help me?~~
Is there a cinema near here?

A [1]__Excuse me, can you help me?__
B Yes, of course.
A [2]________
B No, I'm sorry. There aren't any cinemas near here. But there are two in the city centre.
A [3]________
B Yes, there is. It's in this street. Just over there.
A [4]________
B No problem.

c 05.05 Listen and check.

d Complete the conversation with the words in the box.

any ~~can~~ course for next near no sorry

A Excuse me, [1]__can__ you help me?
B Yes, of [2]________.
A Are there any hotels [3]________ here?
B Yes, there are. There's one in the [4]________ street.
A Oh, good. And are there [5]________ hostels – cheap hostels?
B No, I'm [6]________. There aren't.
A OK. Thanks [7]________ your help.
B [8]________ problem.

e 05.06 Listen and check.

2 PRONUNCIATION
Emphasising what you say 1

a 05.07 Listen to the sentences. Which words are stressed? Tick (✓) the correct box.

1 a ☐ It's a very <u>good</u> hotel.
  b ☑ It's a <u>very</u> good hotel.
2 a ☐ It's <u>so</u> hot today!
  b ☐ It's so hot <u>today</u>!
3 a ☐ I'm <u>really</u> sorry.
  b ☐ I'm really <u>sorry</u>.
4 a ☐ This <u>room's</u> really nice.
  b ☐ This room's <u>really</u> nice.
5 a ☐ It's a very big <u>school</u>.
  b ☐ It's a <u>very</u> big school.
6 a ☐ This TV is <u>so</u> old!
  b ☐ This TV is so <u>old</u>!
7 a ☐ The museum's <u>really</u> boring.
  b ☐ The <u>museum's</u> really boring.
8 a ☐ The car park's very <u>small</u>.
  b ☐ The car park's <u>very</u> small.

5C SKILLS FOR WRITING
It isn't cheap, but it's nice

1 READING

a Read the email. Are the sentences true (*T*) or false (*F*)?

1 The hotel is near the station.
2 Monica and Kalina don't like the hotel.
3 Monica and Kalina like the things in their room.
4 The hotel is expensive.
5 The hotel has a lot of free rooms.
6 Monica and Kalina like the hotel manager.
7 There's a restaurant in the hotel.
8 Monica and Kalina play the guitar in the evening.

Hi Lara,

We're at the Station Hotel. It isn't a big new hotel near the station – it's an old station near the beach! It's great! The rooms are small, but they're very good.

Our room is on the first floor. We have beautiful flowers in the room and there are a lot of pillows and blankets on the beds. It isn't cheap, but we're only here for three nights.

There are a lot of people here. There aren't any free rooms! All the people are very friendly and the manager's nice. In the evenings, we have dinner in the Old Station restaurant. It's in the hotel. The food is good and an old man plays the guitar.

See you soon,

Monica and Kalina

2 WRITING SKILLS *and* and *but*

a Tick (✓) the correct ending for the sentences.

1 I live in Rome, but …
a ☐ I speak Italian.
b ☑ I don't speak Italian.

2 The cinema's big, but …
a ☐ it's very old.
b ☐ it's great.

3 The high school is good and …
a ☐ he'd like to study there.
b ☐ he wouldn't like to study there.

4 The café has great cakes and …
a ☐ it has free wi-fi.
b ☐ it doesn't have free wi-fi.

5 There isn't a bookshop, but …
a ☐ there is a library.
b ☐ there isn't a library.

6 My office is nice and …
a ☐ it isn't near my house.
b ☐ it's near my house.

b Complete the sentences with *and* or *but*.

1 There's a bath ___and___ there's a shower.
2 The room is small ________ it's OK.
3 There's a supermarket in the next street ________ it isn't very big.
4 The city is beautiful ________ it's boring.
5 The hotel has big rooms ________ they're very beautiful.
6 There's a café on the first floor ________ there's a gym on the second floor.
7 It's a beautiful hotel ________ they don't have any free rooms.
8 There's a shower ________ there isn't any hot water!

3 WRITING

a Imagine that you are at a hotel in a new town. Write an email to a friend. Describe the hotel and the town.

Hi ________,

____

____

____

____

____

____

____

____

____

See you soon,

____

UNIT 5
Reading and listening extension

1 READING

a Read the texts. Tick (✓) the things you read about.

1 ☐ a bank
2 ☐ a swimming pool
3 ☐ a cinema
4 ☐ a hospital
5 ☐ a hotel
6 ☐ a car park
7 ☐ a museum
8 ☐ a park
9 ☑ a school
10 ☐ a supermarket

b Read the texts again. Underline the correct words to complete the sentences.

1 *Daria / Geraldo / Elam* lives near a supermarket.
2 *Daria / Geraldo / Elam* doesn't have any children.
3 The hospital is on *Holly Road / High Street / Clarkson Road.*
4 *Holly Road / High Street / Clarkson Road* is a good place to see films.
5 The park is near *Holly Road / High Street / Clarkson Road.*
6 There's a *station / museum / park* near High Street.
7 Daria takes her son to the *swimming pool / ice cream shop / cinema* in the summer.
8 There are a lot of *shops / cafés / offices* near Geraldo's home.

c Write about your street. Think about these questions:

- What is the name of your street?
- Where is your street?
- What is there in or near your street?
- Is it an interesting place to live or work?

MY STREET

I work in the town centre, but I live in Clarkson Road. Clarkson Road isn't near the town centre, but it is a nice place. There are about 60 houses and there's a school, and a shop where I buy bread every day. There's also a little park near the station. It has an ice cream shop and, in summer, I sometimes take my son to the park and we have an ice cream.

1 DARIA

I live on Holly Road with my wife and daughter. It's not a very interesting place to live, but it's easy to get to work because I work at Holly Road Hospital. There are a lot of offices and flats in my road, but there aren't any shops or restaurants. It isn't a problem. There's a big supermarket near Holly Road and there are a lot of buses to the town centre.

2 GERALDO

I live and work on High Street, in the centre of town. There are a lot of different shops and cafés here and there are two bookshops. I work in the bookshop near the museum. When I'm not at work, I sometimes go to the cinema. High Street is a good place to live. My flat is on the first floor and I sometimes sit and watch the people in the street. There is always something interesting to see.

3 ELAM

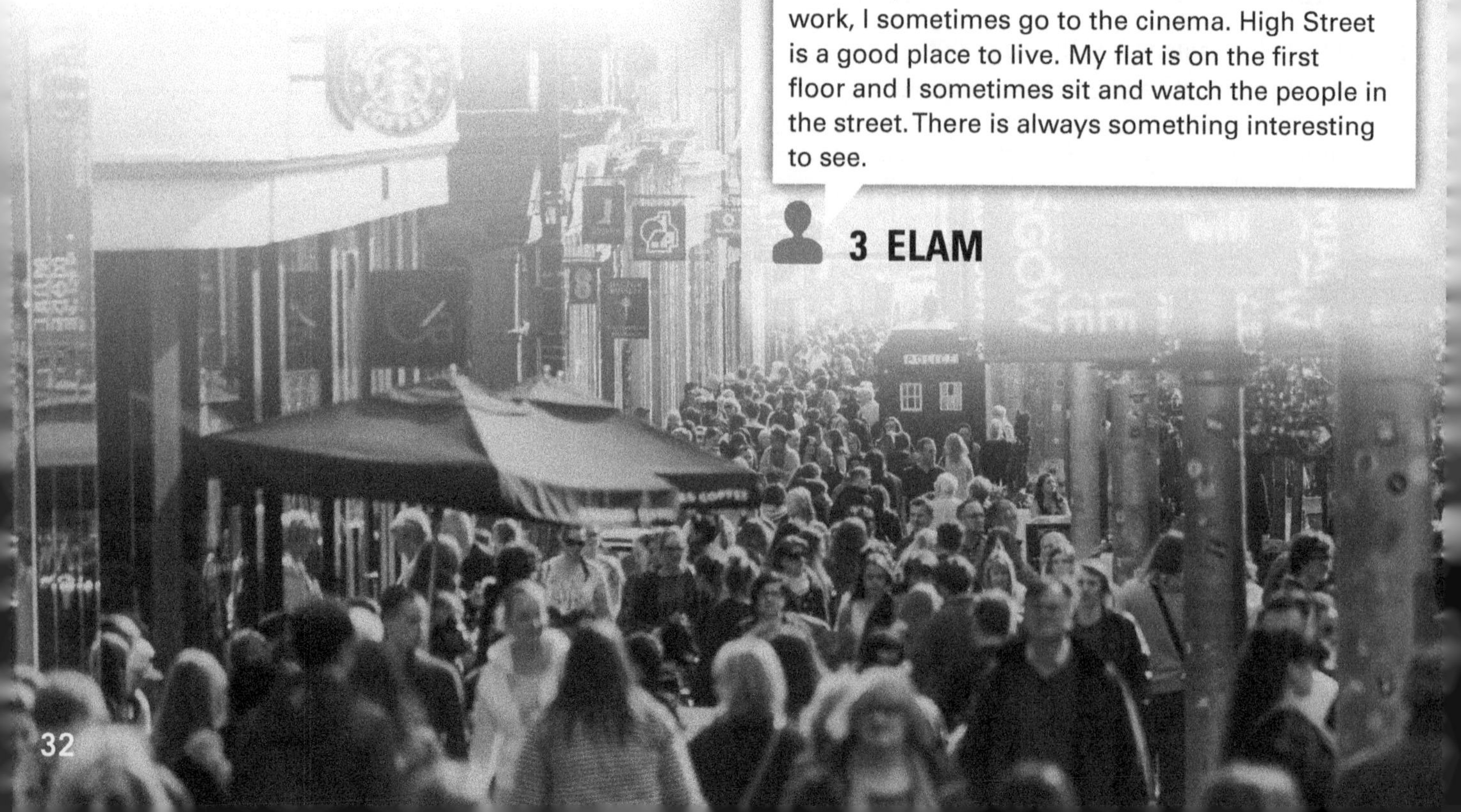

2 LISTENING

a 05.08 Listen to Harry and a receptionist at a tourist office. Are the sentences true (*T*) or false (*F*)?

1 It is summer.
2 There are a lot of free rooms.
3 Harry has a lot of money.
4 Harry chooses a room at the City Hostel.

b 05.08 Listen again. Complete the table with the words in the box.

café cheap friendly expensive free wi-fi
~~near the beach~~ small clean rooms
rooms with baths TVs in rooms free breakfast
near the station rooms with showers

Hotel Casa	City Hostel
near the beach	

c 05.08 Listen again. Underline the correct words.

1 Harry wants a room for a *<u>weekend</u> / week*.
2 The room is for *one person / two people*.
3 He wants to stay near the *station / beach*.
4 Rooms at the Hotel Casa are *$140 / $160*.
5 Single rooms at the City Hostel are *$40 / $60*.
6 There is a café on the *ground / first* floor of the City Hostel.
7 There are *two / three* supermarkets near the hostel.
8 *Harry / The receptionist* phones the hostel.

d Complete the conversation with your own ideas.

RECEPTIONIST Good morning. Can I help?
VISITOR Hi. I'd like a hotel room for ____________ nights near the ____________.
RECEPTIONIST The Grand Hotel is near there. The rooms have ____________ and ____________, and it's ____________ dollars a night.
VISITOR That's very expensive. I don't have a lot of money.
RECEPTIONIST Well, there's the Comfort Hotel in this street. They don't have ____________, but it's cheap.
VISITOR OK.
RECEPTIONIST Do you want me to phone them?
VISITOR Yes, please.

Review

1 GRAMMAR

Tick (✓) the sentences that are correct. Correct the mistakes.

1 ☐ There is a park here?
Is there a park here?
2 ☐ There is two cinemas.
3 ☐ There aren't any supermarkets.
4 ☐ Are there any cafés in this street?
5 ☐ No, there not.
6 ☐ Is there a hotel near here?
7 ☐ Yes, there's.
8 ☐ There not any shops here.

2 VOCABULARY

Correct the spelling.

1 I like this restarant.
I like this restaurant.
2 Where's the scool?
3 Is there a swiming pool?
4 Can I have a blankit, please?
5 There isn't a pilow on the bed.
6 Where's the hospittal?
7 We often go to the beech.
8 Do you have a towl?

REVIEW YOUR PROGRESS

Look again at Review Your Progress on p. 46 of the Student's Book. How well can you do these things now?
3 = very well 2 = well 1 = not so well

I CAN ...	
describe a town	☐
talk about hotels and hostels	☐
ask about and say where places are.	☐

6A I DON'T WORK AT NIGHT

1 GRAMMAR
Present simple: *he / she / it* negative

a Underline the correct words.

1 Shona *don't* / *doesn't* work in an office.
2 I *don't* / *doesn't* work on Wednesdays.
3 Tom doesn't *meet* / *meets* interesting people in his job.
4 We *don't* / *doesn't* speak a lot at work.
5 Mark *don't* / *doesn't* study Italian. He studies Spanish.
6 Selena doesn't *likes* / *like* her job.
7 You *don't* / *doesn't* live here!
8 He *don't* / *doesn't* eat meat.

b Complete the sentences with the correct form of the verbs in brackets.

1 Moira doesn't eat cake, biscuits or ice cream. (not / eat)
2 You ____________ young children. (not / teach)
3 Anton ____________ coffee. (not / like)
4 My brother ____________ in this house. (not / live)
5 My parents ____________. (not / work)
6 Elif ____________ to the cinema with her friends. (not / go)
7 I ____________ his name. (not / know)
8 The doctor ____________ Spanish. (not / speak)

2 VOCABULARY Jobs

a Match the words in the box with the pictures.

chef doctor factory worker football player
office worker receptionist shop assistant
student ~~taxi driver~~ waiter

1 taxi driver

2 ____________

3 ____________

4 ____________

5 ____________

6 ____________

7 ____________

8 ____________

9 ____________

10 ____________

b Underline the correct words.

1 Hello, I'm Natasha. I'm the hotel *assistant* / *receptionist*.
2 **A** What's your brother's job?
B He's a *businessman* / *businesswoman*.
3 I'm an IT *worker* / *player*. I work with computers.
4 I'm a taxi *worker* / *driver*. I sometimes work at night.
5 I work in this restaurant. I'm a *teacher* / *chef*.
6 Lionel Messi is a football *assistant* / *player*.
7 **A** What's your sister's job?
B She a *waiter* / *waitress*.
8 **A** Excuse me! Are you a shop *assistant* / *driver*?
B Yes, I am. Can I help you?

c 06.01 Listen and check.

3 PRONUNCIATION
Sound and spelling: /ɜː/

a 06.02 Listen and tick (✓) the words that have the /ɜː/ sound.

1 park	☐	7 thirty	☐
2 here	☐	8 thirteen	☐
3 girl	☐	9 fruit	☐
4 world	☐	10 Turkey	☐
5 sport	☐	11 wrong	☐
6 work	☐	12 university	☐

6B I WAKE UP AT 4:00

1 GRAMMAR Present simple: *he / she / it* questions

a Put the words in the correct order to make questions.

1 your / up / husband / early / get / does ?
Does your husband get up early?
2 Eduardo / work / does / where ?
______
3 up / does / what / Richard / wake / time ?
______
4 does / feel / how / Ana / work / after ?
______
5 have / home / at / does / breakfast / Alice ?
______
6 what / work / do / your / sister / does / at ?
______

b Complete the sentences with the words in the box.

do Rosa	does she	does your husband
he does	~~does Lottie live~~	Martin get

1 **A** Where *does Lottie live* ?
B In Australia.
2 **A** ______ work at night?
B No, he doesn't.
3 When does ______ home?
4 What time ______ wake up in the morning?
5 When ______ and Luca finish work?
6 **A** Does he study Spanish?
B Yes, ______.

c 06.03 Listen and check.

2 VOCABULARY Daily routine

a Put the daily routine in the correct order.

- [ ] finish work
- [ ] get up
- [ ] go to bed
- [ ] go to work
- [ ] have dinner
- [ ] have lunch
- [ ] start work
- [1] wake up

b Complete the sentences with the verbs in the box.

arrive finish get go (x2) have start ~~wake~~

1 I *wake* up at 7:00 am and I ______ up at 7:15 am.
2 I ______ breakfast at home.
3 I ______ to work every day.
4 I ______ work at 9:00 am and I ______ work at 5:30 pm.
5 I ______ home at 6:30 pm.
6 I ______ to bed at 11:00 pm.

c 06.04 Listen and check.

3 PRONUNCIATION Consonant clusters

a 06.05 Listen and complete the words. Write two letters to make a consonant cluster.

1 *t w* enty
2 _ _ eakfast
3 _ _ anish
4 _ _ ay
5 _ _ uit
6 _ _ ass

6C EVERYDAY ENGLISH
I'll come with you

1 USEFUL LANGUAGE
Making and accepting offers

a Underline the correct words to complete the conversation.

DAN [1]*Do* / ***Would*** you like a cup of tea?
EVA Yes, please.
DAN And [2]*you would* / *would you* like a piece of cake?
EVA No, [3]*OK* / *it's OK*, thanks.
DAN I need to go to the shops for bread.
EVA I'll [4]*can come* / *come* with you.
DAN [5]*That* / *That's* great, thanks. And I need to make some sandwiches.
EVA [6]*I* / *I'll* help you.
DAN Thank you, [7]*it's* / *that's* very kind.

b 06.06 Listen and check.

c Put the conversation in the correct order.

- ☐ **MEG** I need to make lunch for Jake and Carrie.
- ☐ **MEG** And would you like a piece of cake?
- ☐ **MEG** All right. Thanks. We need pizzas.
- ☐ **MEG** Don't worry. It's OK. The pizzas at the supermarket are fine.
- ☐ **MEG** Thank you. That's great.
- [1] **MEG** Would you like a cup of coffee, Rob?
- ☐ **ROB** No, I'm fine, thanks – just coffee, please.
- ☐ **ROB** I'll help you.
- ☐ **ROB** I can make pizzas. I make very good pizzas!
- ☐ **ROB** Yes, please.
- ☐ **ROB** OK, I'll go to the supermarket.

d 06.07 Listen and check.

2 PRONUNCIATION
Emphasising what you say 2

a 06.08 Listen to the sentences. Which words are stressed? Tick (✓) the correct box.

1 **A** I need to make dinner for eight people!
B a ☐ I **can** help you.
b ☑ **I** can help you.

2 **A** I need to go to the supermarket, but I'm really busy.
B a ☐ I'll **go**.
b ☐ **I'll** go.

3 **A** Oh no! I don't have any money with me!
B a ☐ **I** can pay.
b ☐ I can **pay**.

4 **A** I can't open this bottle of water!
B a ☐ **I'll** do it.
b ☐ I'll **do** it.

5 **A** I need to go to the shops. Can you drive me?
B a ☐ Sorry, but I'm really busy. Jim can take **you**.
b ☐ Sorry, but I'm really busy. **Jim** can take you.

6 **A** I need some cups. Do you have any cups?
B a ☐ No, I don't. **I** can give you some glasses.
b ☐ No, I don't. I can give you some **glasses**.

6C SKILLS FOR WRITING
She's a taxi driver because she likes driving

1 READING

a Read the email and tick (✓) the correct answers.

Hi Mum,

Life here in New York is exciting!

I have a job in a café in Manhattan. I get up at half past four in the morning every day from Monday to Saturday and I work from half past five until two o'clock in the afternoon.

There are a lot of people in the café from six until nine o'clock because the breakfasts are great! I really like the breakfasts! The sandwiches are also really good and I have lunch there every day.

I have a new friend in New York. His name's Rex and he's a taxi driver. He often works at night and he has breakfast in the café at half past five. He always says, 'Coffee and breakfast for dinner, please!' Then he goes home and he goes to bed.

Email me soon!

Love,
Ivan

1 Where does Ivan work?
   a ☐ in a restaurant
   b ☐ in a shop
   c ☑ in a café
2 What time does Ivan get up?
   a ☐ 4:30 am
   b ☐ 5:30 am
   c ☐ 6:30 am
3 Ivan doesn't work on ________.
   a ☐ Mondays
   b ☐ Saturdays
   c ☐ Sundays
4 What time does Ivan start work?
   a ☐ 5:30 am
   b ☐ 9:00 am
   c ☐ 2:00 pm
5 Ivan likes ________ at the café.
   a ☐ the breakfasts
   b ☐ the sandwiches
   c ☐ the breakfasts and the sandwiches
6 Rex goes to the café at 5:30 am because he ________.
   a ☐ always starts work at 6:00 am
   b ☐ often finishes work in the morning
   c ☐ works at the café

2 WRITING SKILLS *because* and *also*

a Correct the mistakes.

1 Diana's a taxi driver. Because she likes driving.
   Diana's a taxi driver because she likes driving.
2 They have breakfast at school. They have also lunch at school.
   ____
3 I study business at university. I also am a waiter.
   ____
4 She gets up early. She goes also to bed early.
   ____
5 He's a teacher because he gets up early.
   ____
6 She sometimes works at night. Because she's a doctor.
   ____

b Complete the sentences with *also* or *because*.

1 There's a museum in my home town. There's ___also___ a cinema.
2 She speaks Turkish ________ her mum's from Turkey.
3 I play football. I ________ play tennis.
4 He goes to bed at 8 am ________ he works at night.
5 My parents have a cat ________ they love animals.
6 I have black hair. My brother ________ has black hair.

3 WRITING

a Write an email about the daily routine of one of your friends or a member of your family. Use the email in exercise 1 to help you.

____
____
____
____
____
____
____
____
____

UNIT 6
Reading and listening extension

1 READING

a Read the magazine article. Complete the sentences with the words in the box.

at night	in the afternoon	in the evening
in the morning	at the weekend	

1 Claudia sees her friends ______________.
2 She has classes at the university ______________.
3 She goes to the university library ______________.
4 From Monday to Friday, she goes to work ______________.
5 She works until 11:30 ______________.

b Read the article again. Are the sentences true (*T*) or false (*F*)?

1 Claudia studies in her home country.
2 Claudia likes her course.
3 Her classes start at 8 am.
4 She doesn't go home in the afternoon.
5 She has dinner at home.
6 She goes to work after dinner.
7 She finishes work at 11:30.
8 She works all weekend.

c Write a short description of your day. Think about these questions:

- What time do you get up and go to bed?
- What do you do in the morning, afternoon and evening?
- When do you see your friends?

University *Life*

University is expensive in the USA and students also need to pay for course books, food and a place to live. A lot of students work to get extra money. Is it a good idea?

We ask a student.

Claudia, 23

I'm a student in New York, but I'm from Barcelona. I love my course, but New York is expensive, so I work in a cinema in the evenings and on Saturdays.

My day usually starts at 7:45 am when I get up and have breakfast. Then I go to my classes at the university. They start at 9:00 am and finish at 12:30 pm. There aren't any classes in the afternoon so I study in the university library. I have something to eat in the student restaurant and I walk to the cinema. My working hours are 6:00 pm to 11:30 pm from Monday to Friday, and 1:30 pm to 11:30 pm on Saturdays. Sunday is my free day and I play tennis or go to a museum with my friends.

My job is OK, but I don't want to work six days a week. I get home late and I only get six or seven hours' sleep. Sometimes, I feel very tired in my classes and I want to sleep, which isn't good.

2 LISTENING

a 06.09 Listen to the interview. Underline the correct answers.

1 Ian Baker is *Scottish / English.*
2 He is a *factory worker / businessman.*
3 Ian is *single / married.*
4 Ian and Rita have a factory in *Aberdeen / Glasgow.*
5 *Eighty / Ninety* people work in the factory.
6 Their customers are in *Europe / Asia* and South America.

b 06.09 Listen again and underline the correct words.

1 Ian and Rita *have / don't have* a computer factory in Scotland.
2 The factory *makes / doesn't make* computers for hospitals.
3 Ian *works / doesn't work* about 12 hours a day.
4 Ian *sits / doesn't sit* in his office every day.
5 Ian *meets / doesn't meet* the people who use his computers.
6 Ian and Rita *have / don't have* customers in the UK.
7 Ian *speaks / doesn't speak* a foreign language.
8 Rita *goes / doesn't go* to South America with Ian.

c Complete the conversation with your own ideas.

INTERVIEWER Welcome to the show. This week, we're talking to people who live and work in ____________. Today, my guest is ____________. Where in ____________ do you live?
GUEST I live in ____________.
INTERVIEWER And what do you do?
GUEST I'm a(n) ____________.
INTERVIEWER That's interesting. Do you like your work?
GUEST ____________ because ____________.
INTERVIEWER Do you work long hours?
GUEST ____________.
INTERVIEWER And do you visit places for work?
GUEST ____________.
INTERVIEWER Thanks very much for talking to us today.

Review

1 GRAMMAR

Correct the mistakes.

1 Lee doesn't works on Mondays.
Lee doesn't work on Mondays.
2 Does he speaks English?
3 When Anna arrives home?
4 Pedro like fish?
5 Seb not plays tennis.
6 **A** Does Becky live here?
B Yes, she lives.
7 **A** Does Russell have a computer?
B No, he not.
8 Where she lives?

2 VOCABULARY

Tick (✓) the sentences that are correct. Correct the mistakes.

1 ☑ I wake up at 6:30 am.
2 ☐ He gets up at 6:30 am.
3 ☐ She's a driver taxi.
4 ☐ I have a lunch at work.
5 ☐ He's a businesman.
6 ☐ She's a chef.
7 ☐ I'm a receptionist.
8 ☐ I go bed at 11:00 pm.

REVIEW YOUR PROGRESS

Look again at Review Your Progress on p. 54 of the Student's Book. How well can you do these things now?
3 = very well 2 = well 1 = not so well

I CAN ...	
talk about people's jobs	☐
talk about daily routines and habits	☐
make and accept offers.	☐

7A I LIKE THIS LAMP

1 GRAMMAR *this, that, these, those*

a Complete the sentences with the words in the box.

this that these those

1 Do you like ______ flowers?

2 Do you like ______ flowers?

3 I'd like ______ car.

4 I want ______ car!

b 07.01 Listen and check.

c Complete the sentences with *this, that, these* or *those*. Remember *near* = here (near me) and *far* = there (not near me).

1 ___That___ picture's interesting. (far)
2 ______ plates are nice. (near)
3 I like ______ chair. (near)
4 How much is ______ guitar? (far)
5 I like ______ shop. (near)
6 ______ bags are beautiful. (far)
7 I don't like ______ lamp. (far)
8 How much are ______ speakers? (near)

2 VOCABULARY Common objects 2

a Complete the sentences with the words in the box.

book glass ~~clock~~ ball guitar picture plant plate speakers suitcase

1 What time is it? There isn't a ___clock___ in this room.
2 Can I have a ______ for this pizza, please?
3 Would you like a ______ of water?
4 I have a lot of clothes, but this bag's very small. I need a big ______.
5 I have a great ______ of my family. Do you want to see it?
6 This is my English ______. It's called *Empower*.
7 Stafano teaches music to children. He often takes his ______ to school for music lessons.
8 My new car stereo has great ______. The sound is really good!
9 What's that ______ in the garden? Its flowers are very nice.
10 We want to play football, but we don't have a ______.

3 VOCABULARY Prices

a Tick (✓) the correct words.

1 This glass is €10.50.
a [ ] ten euros and fifty
b [✓] ten euros fifty
c [ ] one hundred and five euros

2 This football is £30.
a [ ] thirty pound
b [ ] thirteen pounds
c [ ] thirty pounds

3 That guitar is $129.99
a [ ] one hundred and ninety-nine dollars
b [ ] one hundred and twenty-nine dollars ninety-nine
c [ ] one hundred and nine-twenty dollars nine-ninety

4 That picture is €24.75.
a [ ] twenty-four euros seventy-five
b [ ] forty-two euros seventy-five
c [ ] seventy-five euros and twenty-four

5 Those cups are £9.50.
a [ ] ninety-five pounds
b [ ] nine pounds fifty
c [ ] five pounds ninety

6 These plants are $3.89.
a [ ] three dollars eighty-nine
b [ ] three dollar eighty-nine
c [ ] three of dollars eighty-nine

b 07.02 Listen and check.

4 PRONUNCIATION Sound and spelling: /b/, /p/, /g/ and /k/

a 07.03 Listen to the words. Write the missing letters.

1 ball
2 suit_ase
3 _lass
4 _a_
5 _late
6 lam_
7 _uitar
8 _oo_
9 _up
10 _lant

7B IT'S GREG'S T-SHIRT

1 GRAMMAR
Possessive *'s*; Revision of adverbs

a Put the words in the correct order to make sentences. Add an apostrophe (') where needed. There may be more than one possible answer.

1 bag / it's / Kates .
It's Kate's bag.
2 Peters / they're / jeans .
____
3 brown / friends / jacket / is / my .
____
4 the / are / new / boys / trousers .
____
5 I / hat / never / wear / a .
____
6 clothes / I / my / sisters / sometimes / wear .
____

b 07.04 Listen and check.

c Complete the sentences with the names and nouns in brackets and the possessive *'s*.

1 This is *Anna's* T-shirt. (Anna)
2 Where's ______________ phone? (Mehmet)
3 I like ______________ new house. (Juan and Laura)
4 That's ______________ computer. (the girls)
5 What's ______________ phone number? (Preeda)
6 I like ______________ shoes. (the children)

2 VOCABULARY Clothes and colours

a Complete the sentences with the words in the box.

black blue brown green ~~grey~~ red white yellow

1 Older people often have *grey* hair.
2 Chocolate is usually ______________.
3 Bananas are ______________.
4 Milk is ______________.
5 Strawberries are ______________.
6 Grass is ______________.
7 A tiger is orange and ______________.
8 On a sunny day, the sky is ______________.

b Complete the crossword puzzle.

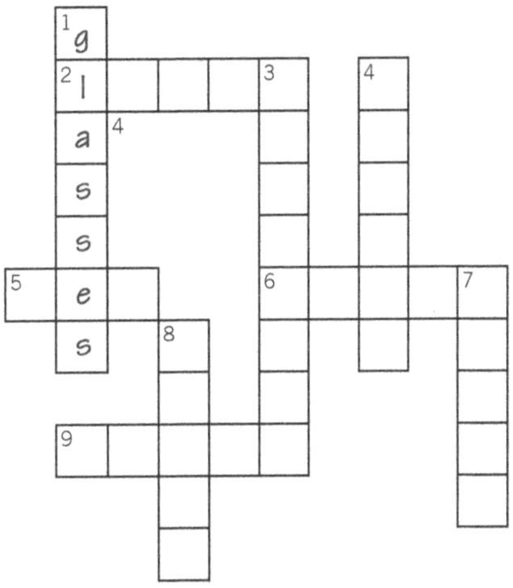

→ Across
2 The opposite of 'dark'.
5 ______________ + white = pink.
6 It's difficult to walk in these ______________! They're very big!
9 These are usually blue. You wear them on your legs. They come from the USA.

↓ Down
1 I wear *glasses* to read a book or use the computer.
3 You wear ______________ on your legs.
4 Eggs are white and ______________.
7 Men wear this to work. They wear it on their body.
8 Old photos are ______________ and white.

3 PRONUNCIATION
Sound and spelling: /ʃ/ and /dʒ/

a 07.05 Listen to the words in the box. What sound do the **marked** letters have? Complete the table.

~~jeans~~ lar**g**e fa**sh**ion **sh**oes interna**t**ional **J**apanese
ve**g**etables **sh**irt **G**ermany **s**ugar villa**g**e **sh**op

/ʃ/ (e.g., ***sh**e*)	/dʒ/ (e.g., *chan**g**e*)
	jeans

7C EVERYDAY ENGLISH
Can I help you?

1 USEFUL LANGUAGE Going shopping

a Complete the conversations with the sentences in the box.

Here's your receipt. Can I look around? ~~Enter your PIN, please.~~ I'd like that T-shirt, please. How much are these bags?

1 **A** That's £52.95, please.
B Can I use a card to pay?
A Yes. Enter your PIN, please.

2 **A** Can I help you?
B ______________________
A Of course.

3 **A** ______________________
B Thanks.

4 **A** ______________________
B They're £35 each.

5 **A** ______________________
B Certainly. Here you are.

b 07.06 Listen and check.

c Put the conversation in the correct order.

☐ **SHOP ASSISTANT** Thank you.
1 **SHOP ASSISTANT** Can I help you?
☐ **SHOP ASSISTANT** Certainly. That's £16, please.
☐ **SHOP ASSISTANT** They're £4 each.
☐ **SHOP ASSISTANT** OK, here you are.
☐ **SHOP ASSISTANT** Of course. Enter your PIN, please. OK, here's your receipt. Would you like a bag?
☐ **CUSTOMER** OK, I'd like four white plates, please.
☐ **CUSTOMER** Can I use a card to pay?
☐ **CUSTOMER** Thank you very much.
☐ **CUSTOMER** No, don't worry.
☐ **CUSTOMER** Yes, how much are these white plates?

d 07.07 Listen and check.

2 PRONUNCIATION Connected speech

a 07.08 Listen to the sentences. What are the extra sounds? Tick (✓) the correct box.

	/j/	/w/
1 Here you‿are.		✓
2 Is it blue‿or green?		
3 Three‿apples, please.		
4 Are you‿OK?		
5 She‿only wears white.		
6 These cups are for me‿and you.		
7 He‿always wears black.		
8 There are two‿empty bags.		

7C SKILLS FOR WRITING
Good prices!

1 READING

a Read the messages in the table 1–6. Which advertisement A–D is each message about? Tick (✓) the correct box.

Ⓐ **FOR SALE**
Old books, photos, magazines and newspapers. Very interesting! Good prices.

Ⓑ **FOR SALE**
Beautiful 1960s plates, cups, bowls and glasses. Not expensive!

Ⓒ **FOR SALE**
Bed, tables and chairs. I also have some great lamps and pictures for sale.

Ⓓ **FOR SALE**
Men's trousers, shirts, jackets and coats. Very good condition! I also have shoes, umbrellas and watches for sale.

	A	B	C	D
1 You have an online advertisement for men's clothes. Do you also sell women's clothes?				✓
2 I saw your online advertisement for a bed. I'd like to buy it!				
3 I saw your advertisement. You have some interesting things for sale. How much is the watch? Is it old or new?				
4 I saw your ad for things you want to sell. I'd like to see a photo of the bowls, please.				
5 I have a few questions about the things in your ad. Are the photos in colour or black and white? Do you have any magazines in other languages? How old are the newspapers?				
6 I saw your advertisement and I need four chairs for my flat. How many do you have? How old are they?				

2 WRITING SKILLS
Commas, exclamation marks and question marks

a Tick (✓) the correct ending for the sentences.

1 How much is the …
a ☐ plant, b ☐ plant! c ☑ plant?

2 Good …
a ☐ prices, b ☐ prices! c ☐ prices?

3 Hats for sale: we have …
a ☐ red white green blue and yellow
b ☐ red, white, green, blue, and yellow,
c ☐ red, white, green, blue and yellow.

4 Can I pay …
a ☐ online, b ☐ online! c ☐ online?

5 Beautiful …
a ☐ bags, and shoes.
b ☐ bags and shoes.
c ☐ bags! and shoes!

6 I'd like to buy …
a ☐ a picture, a bowl, a lamp and a book.
b ☐ a picture, a bowl, a lamp and a book?
c ☐ a picture, a bowl a lamp and a book

7 How old is …
a ☐ it, b ☐ it! c ☐ it?

8 We need some …
a ☐ cups, plates and glasses.
b ☐ cups plates and glasses.
c ☐ cups, plates, and glasses?

b Add commas, exclamation marks or question marks to the sentences.

1 How old are you
How old are you?

2 You're a grandmother
____

3 I have a sandwich a drink and a banana.
____

4 These shoes are very expensive
____

5 Where is the station
____

6 Satoko Carolina and Beto are in my class.
____

3 WRITING

a Write a reply to this advertisement. You have a new home and you need furniture, a TV and a computer.

FURNITURE FOR SALE!
We have chairs, tables, clocks and technology items for sale.
Good condition! Contact Jack. **Reply to this ad**

Hi Jack,
____
____
____
____
____

Thanks,
____

UNIT 7
Reading and listening extension

1 READING

a Read the article and match topics a–d to paragraphs 1–4.

a ☐ What I wear when I'm not at work
b ☐ Where I buy my clothes
c ☐ What I wear for special occasions
d ☐ My work clothes

b Read the article again. Are the sentences true (*T*) or false (*F*)?

1 Martin's uniform is blue.
2 The police officers' yellow jackets are useful.
3 Martin's friends like fashionable clothes.
4 His favourite colour is brown.
5 He has an expensive suit for special events.
6 He usually wears a dark grey shirt for special events.
7 H&M is in the shopping mall.
8 Luciana's favourite shop is the same as Martin's.

c Choose someone you know. Write a description of their clothes. Think about these questions:

- What clothes do they wear at different times of the day and different days of the week?
- What are their favourite colours?
- Where do they buy their clothes?

MY CLOTHES by Martin López

1 I don't have to worry about my work clothes. I'm a police officer and I have a uniform. I like the uniform. We wear a dark blue jacket, dark blue trousers and a white shirt. We also have big yellow police jackets to wear when we're outside in the street. These jackets are very useful because people can see that we are police officers.

2 I'm not very interested in fashion. My wife Luciana says that my clothes are boring, but most of my friends' clothes are the same as mine! When I'm not at work, I like to wear comfortable clothes, for example, jeans and a T-shirt or a jumper. I don't really have a favourite colour, but I try not to wear dark blue because it's the colour of my uniform. My favourite item of clothing is my old brown jacket.

3 I don't have many expensive clothes, but sometimes I go to special events, for example, when friends get married and I need to wear something nice. I have a suit by the designer Tom Ford. It has dark grey trousers and a matching jacket. I usually wear this with a white shirt and tie.

4 I usually go shopping with Luciana. We both like to go to the shopping mall in the centre of town. It has a lot of shops and it's easy to find things. My favourite shop there is H&M. The clothes in H&M are usually comfortable and they aren't very expensive. I buy all my clothes there, but Luciana's favourite shop is Urban Outfitters.

2 LISTENING

a 07.09 Listen to the conversation. What does the shop sell? Underline the correct answer.

books bags computers birthday cards
things for the home clothes chocolates

b 07.09 Listen again. Tick (✓) the things the people talk about.

1 a birthday ☑
2 a holiday ☐
3 a party ☐
4 a parent ☐
5 a present ☐
6 a friend ☐
7 a new flat ☐
8 a new car ☐
9 a birthday card ☐
10 a postcard ☐

c 07.09 Listen again and underline the correct words.

1 Paul thinks shopping is *tiring* / *boring*.
2 Sue wants to buy something *useful* / *colourful*.
3 The cups have pictures of *flowers* / *animals* on them.
4 The lamp is *blue* / *brown*.
5 Paul doesn't like the *colour* / *price* of the lamp.
6 Paul's mum wants a table for her *TV* / *laptop*.
7 The table is *£50* / *£60*.
8 Next, Paul and Sue will go to a *café* / *card shop*.

d Write about a shop you like. Think about these questions:

- What's the shop's name?
- Where is it?
- What things do you buy there?
- How often do you go there?
- Why do you like it?

Review

1 GRAMMAR

Tick (✓) the sentences that are correct. Correct the mistakes. Remember *near* = here (near me) and *far* = there (not near me).

1 ☑ How much is this chair? (near)
2 ☐ This cups are £6. (near)
3 ☐ That bag is nice. (far)
4 ☐ Those picture is interesting. (far)
5 ☐ I like Martins shoes.
6 ☐ I have two boys. This is the boys' bedroom.
7 ☐ I have one daughter. This is my daughter's hat.
8 ☐ It's Anna's and David's computer.

2 VOCABULARY

Correct the mistakes.

1 I'd like a yellow suitcais.
I'd like a yellow suitcase.
2 He has a red giutar.
3 This pikture is one hundred and sixty-three pounds.
4 Do you have any speekers?
5 It's a light brawn skirt.
6 Where's your green jaket?
7 I have six wite shirts.
8 It's a grey dark coat.

REVIEW YOUR PROGRESS

Look again at Review Your Progress on p. 62 of the Student's Book. How well can you do these things now?
3 = very well 2 = well 1 = not so well

I CAN ...	
talk about things I want to buy	☐
talk about the clothes that people wear	☐
ask about and pay for things in a shop.	☐

8A I WAS ON TOUR WITH MY BAND

1 GRAMMAR Past simple: *be*

a Put the words in the correct order to make sentences and questions.

1 last / concert / at / night / was / I / a .
I was at a concert last night.
2 where / morning / this / Nina / was ?
______
3 weren't / last / we / at / night / concert / the .
______
4 they / ago / in / week / were / a / Bologna .
______
5 week / were / Mexico City / you / in / last ?
______
6 were / yes, / we .
______
7 the / afternoon / at / meeting / was / this / Adrian ?
______
8 no, / wasn't / he .
______

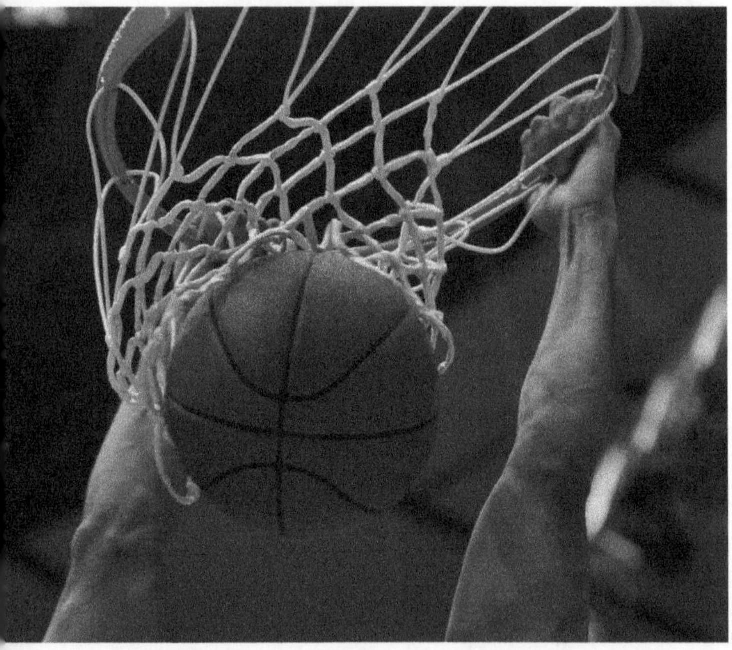

b Complete the conversation with *was, were, weren't* or *wasn't.*

A You [1] *weren't* here on Friday afternoon. Where [2]______ you?
B I [3]______ with my brothers. We [4]______ at a basketball game.
A Oh, [5]______ it good?
B No, it [6]______. I don't like basketball.
A Oh. And where [7]______ you on Friday evening?
B We [8]______ at a party.
A [9]______ it a good party?
B It [10]______ OK. The people [11]______ really nice, but the music [12]______ very good.

c 08.01 Listen and check.

2 VOCABULARY Past time expressions

a Complete the sentences with the words in the box.

~~a year ago~~	last month	last night
this afternoon	this morning	yesterday

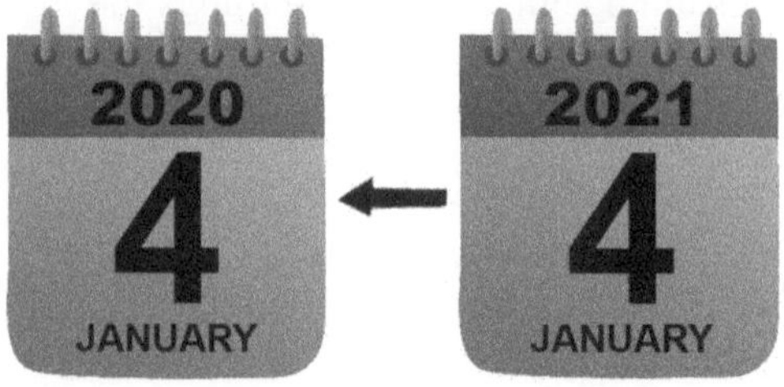

1 It's January 2021. It was January 2020 *a year ago*.
2 Today it's Monday, the fourth of January. ______, it was the third of January.
3 It's Monday evening. I was at work from 2:00 pm until 5:30 pm. I was at work ______.
4 It's Monday evening. I was at work from 8:30 am until 11:30 am. I was at work ______.
5 It's Monday. I was at work from 8:00 pm until 11:30 pm on Sunday. I was at work ______.
6 It's January 2021. I was in Brazil in December 2020. I was in Brazil ______.

b 08.02 Listen and check.

c Underline the correct words.

1 I was in Sydney *at* / *on* / *ago* Thursday.
2 **A** Were you in Montreal *yesterday* / *this yesterday* / *on yesterday*?
B Yes, I was.
3 Was Elif at work *on* / *this* / *last* morning?
4 They weren't at home *last* / *ago* weekend.
5 We were at a concert *the last night* / *on last night* / *last night.*
6 Where were you *three months ago* / *ago three months* / *last three months*?

3 PRONUNCIATION *was / were*

a 08.03 Listen and underline the two stressed words in each sentence.

1 James was at home.
2 We were in Brighton.
3 You were at work.
4 My parents were in Australia.
5 The party was fun.
6 The match was exciting.
7 The concert was good.
8 The meetings were interesting.

8B HE SAW A BEAR

1 GRAMMAR Past simple: positive

a Complete the crossword puzzle with the past simple form of the verbs.

→ Across
2 see
4 look
5 watch
8 come
9 eat
10 have

↓ Down
1 jump
3 walk
5 go
6 try
7 hear
8 call

b Complete the story with the past simple form of the verbs in brackets.

A Great Evening

My friend Andrés and I ¹ *arrived* (arrive) at the cinema at 5:30 pm and we ²__________ (watch) a film. In the film, a man ³__________ (play) a video game and the video game ⁴__________ (try) to change him into a robot. It was really interesting!

Then we ⁵__________ (go) to the new café on King Street. I ⁶__________ (see) Oscar, a man I know from work. We asked him to eat with us and he ⁷__________ (say) yes. Oscar ⁸__________ (hear) about the film and we ⁹__________ (talk) about it. Andrés went home at about 8:30 pm but Oscar and I ¹⁰__________ (stay) at the café and ¹¹__________ (have) coffee.

After that, we went to my house and ¹²__________ (play) cards. It was a great evening.

2 VOCABULARY Free time activities

a Complete the activities with the words in the box.

go (x2) have (x2) listen to play (x2) read watch

1 *play* the guitar

2 __________ music

3 __________ a shower

4 __________ to the cinema

5 __________ a glass of water

6 __________ a magazine

7 __________ a video game

8 __________ a football match

9 __________ shopping

b Underline the correct words.

1 I *listen to* / *<u>read</u>* / *go* the news online every day.
2 I sometimes *go* / *listen to* / *watch* films on my phone.
3 I never *go* / *have* / *watch* to the cinema.
4 I don't *listen to* / *play* / *read* magazines.
5 I *go* / *have* / *play* a shower every evening.
6 I usually *listen to* / *read* / *watch* a podcast in the morning.
7 I often *read* / *play* / *watch* football matches on TV.
8 I *have* / *play* / *watch* video games every day.
9 I always *have* / *listen to* / *watch* music in the evening.
10 I always *go* / *play* / *watch* to parties at the weekend.

c ▶ 08.04 Listen and check.

3 PRONUNCIATION Sound and spelling: /t/ and /d/

a ▶ 08.05 Listen to the past simple verbs. Is the final sound /t/ or /d/? Tick (✓) the correct box.

	/t/	/d/
1 talked	✓	☐
2 called	☐	☐
3 tried	☐	☐
4 listened	☐	☐
5 played	☐	☐
6 watched	☐	☐
7 looked	☐	☐
8 lived	☐	☐

8C EVERYDAY ENGLISH

Let's go somewhere this weekend

1 USEFUL LANGUAGE
Making and responding to suggestions

a Complete the sentences and questions with the words in the box.

could free ~~idea~~ let's shall

1 That's a nice *idea*.
2 ____________ go to that new restaurant.
3 ____________ we go to the cinema?
4 I'm not ____________ on Tuesday.
5 We ____________ go swimming.

b Underline the correct words to complete the conversation.

ANGELA I went to the beach last week. It was great.
SOL Oh, 1 *let* / *let's* go to the beach together sometime!
ANGELA 2 *That's* / *This is* a lovely idea.
SOL We 3 *could* / *shall* go this weekend.
ANGELA I'm sorry, I'm 4 *free* / *busy* with my family this weekend.
SOL OK. 5 *Shall we* / *We shall* go next Saturday?
ANGELA I 6 *can't* / *don't* go on Saturday, but I'm 7 *free* / *busy* on Sunday. I can go on Sunday.
SOL 8 *Nice* / *OK*, Sunday. Good.
ANGELA Great!

c 08.06 Listen and check.

d Put the conversation in the correct order.

☐ **DAVID** Great! Let's go now.
☐ **DAVID** OK, that's a nice idea! See you at eleven.
☐ **DAVID** OK. We could go at eleven o'clock.
1 **DAVID** Shall we go for a coffee?
☐ **KYOKO** Great! Shall we go to the new Italian café?
☐ **KYOKO** Coffee? Good idea!
☐ **KYOKO** I'm sorry, I can't go now. I have a meeting at ten o'clock.

e 08.07 Listen and check.

2 PRONUNCIATION
Main stress and intonation

a 08.08 Listen to the sentences. Does the intonation rise (↗) or fall (↘) after the underlined main stress? Tick (✓) the correct box.

	↗	↘
1 Shall we go for a meal tomorrow?		✓
2 That's a lovely idea.		
3 Let's go to the cinema next week.		
4 That's a great idea.		
5 I'm away on Tuesday.		
6 That's a nice idea.		

8C SKILLS FOR WRITING
I want to say thank you

1 READING

a Read the thank you note and texts. Complete the sentences with the names in the box.

~~Charlie~~	Isla	Elena	Nina	Oliver	Rai

1 ___Charlie___ helped a friend with her flat.
2 __________ drove to hospital.
3 __________ helped a friend at the shops.
4 __________ needed to go to hospital.
5 __________ bought things for her flat.
6 __________ bought a new dress.

Dear Isla,

Thank you for your help on Wednesday. It was fun to go shopping together and you helped me find a really nice dress. Now I need some shoes!

See you soon,

Nina

Hi Charlie,
I want to say thanks for your help last weekend. The new table and chairs look really good. I bought some big pictures and lamps on Monday. I hope you can come for dinner some time!
Thanks!

Elena

Hi Oliver,
Here are some chocolates to say thank you for driving me to hospital on Monday. You were great! I'm home again now, but I'm in bed for a few days. I hope we can meet for a coffee soon.

Rai

2 WRITING SKILLS
Writing short emails, notes and texts

a Underline the correct words to complete the email.

[1]*At / For / Dear* Olivia,

I [2]*want / was / would want* to say thank you [3]*to / about / for* coming to my concert on Friday. I hope you liked the music. It [4]*be / was / is* good to meet your friends. [5]*I'd like / I hope / I want* we can meet again soon. [6]*There / Here are / Here were* some photos of the evening. I really like the picture of you and Ali!

[7]*See / Talk / Best* you soon,

Ava

b Match 1–6 with a–f to make expressions.

1 [d] Dear
2 [ ] Here are
3 [ ] Thanks for
4 [ ] I hope we can
5 [ ] See you
6 [ ] Talk to

a some photos of the party.
b soon.
c you later!
d Tony,
e see each other again soon.
f your note.

3 WRITING

a Imagine you had lunch at a friend's house. Write a thank you email to your friend. Remember to give information about:

- the lunch you had
- the people you met
- your photos of the day
- when you hope to see your friend again.

Hi __________,

____

____

____

____

____

____

____

____

____

Talk to you later!

UNIT 8
Reading and listening extension

1 READING

a Read Giulia's blog. Are the sentences true or false?

1 Giulia was at work on Friday.
2 She lives with Emma and Sara.
3 She was in her office on Sunday.
4 She had a coffee with Marta on Sunday.
5 Emma and Sara went to Cagliari on Monday.
6 Giulia and Marta travelled to the airport together.

b Read the blog again. Underline the correct words to complete the sentences.

1 Giulia had a *good* / *bad* day at work on Friday.
2 She *went to the theatre* / *stayed at home* on Friday evening.
3 She missed the end of the film because she was *tired* / *bored*.
4 She *watched a cookery programme* / *cooked a Mexican meal* on Sunday.
5 Marta bought *a suitcase* / *some books* on Sunday.
6 Giulia and her friends had pizza for *lunch* / *dinner* on Sunday.
7 They were in the pizza restaurant for *three* / *four* hours.
8 Giulia got up *early* / *late* on Monday.
9 Giulia and Marta arrived in Cagliari at *7:30* / *8:30* on Monday.
10 They were in Cagliari *for a holiday* / *on business*.

c Write a blog about your daily life. Write about last week. Think about these questions:

- What did you do?
- Where did you go?
- Who did you see?

80%

FRIDAY 9TH JAN

I had a bad day at work. The office was really busy. I was so happy to get home. My roommates, Emma and Sara, wanted me to go to the theatre with them, but I was tired. They went out, but I watched an old film on TV in my bedroom. It had a great story, but I fell asleep and don't know how it ended.

SUNDAY 11TH JAN

I got up late and had a long bath. Then I watched a programme about Mexican cookery. I was hungry after the programme, so I made a cheese sandwich – my favourite! I met Marta in town for a coffee and then we went shopping. I bought a suitcase for our holiday in Cagliari and Marta got some books. At 6:00, we met Emma and Sara for a pizza. We were in the restaurant until 10:00!

MONDAY 12TH JAN

I got up at 4:00 this morning. I was really tired, but our plane to Cagliari was at 6:30. I went to the airport in a taxi. Marta was already there with the tickets. It only took an hour to travel from Rome to Cagliari. We had breakfast on the plane. Then Marta read one of her new books and I looked out the window. We had a tour of Cagliari today and now we're at our hotel. It's lovely!

2 LISTENING

a 08.09 Listen to the conversation. Complete the text with the words in the box.

Barcelona	the beach	a concert	work
a restaurant	a museum	~~home~~	the park

Matt

Matt was at 1 *home* with his children on Saturday, but his wife was at 2 ________. On Sunday, they all went to 3 ________ in 4 ________.

Grace

Grace and her sister were in 5 ________ at the weekend. They went to 6 ________ on 7 ________ on Saturday and to 8 ________ on Sunday.

b 08.09 Listen again. Who says the sentences? Write *Matt* or *Grace*.

1 I think they were a bit bored. *Matt*
2 ... it wasn't very cold ... ________
3 There were a lot of people. ________
4 The bands were really good. ________
5 The restaurant was empty! ________
6 A family ticket was only £10.00! ________
7 There weren't any other people. ________
8 It was really interesting. ________
9 There was a lot to see and do. ________
10 It was free. ________

c Write an email to a friend about last weekend. Remember to say:

- where you were
- who you were with
- what you did.

Review

1 GRAMMAR

Correct the mistakes.

1 I am in a meeting yesterday afternoon.
I was in a meeting yesterday afternoon.
2 Carlota not was at work yesterday.
3 We are in the USA in 2018.
4 Where they were yesterday?
5 We was play tennis.
6 Jess arrivd at nine o'clock.
7 I did have breakfast this morning.
8 Carrie goed to London last year.

2 VOCABULARY

Tick (✓) the sentences that are correct. Correct the mistakes.

1 ☐ Where were you ago five years?
Where were you five years ago?
2 ☐ I saw George the last week.
3 ☐ We had a meeting on Monday.
4 ☐ Olivia was here at the weekend.
5 ☐ They listened music last night.
6 ☐ I had a shower this morning.
7 ☐ We played video games at the weekend.
8 ☐ We went the cinema yesterday.

REVIEW YOUR PROGRESS

Look again at Review Your Progress on p. 70 of the Student's Book. How well can you do these things now?
3 = very well 2 = well 1 = not so well

I CAN ...	
talk about past events	☐
describe events in the past	☐
make and respond to suggestions.	☐

9A I DIDN'T STAY IN A HOTEL

1 GRAMMAR Past simple: negative

a Underline the correct words to complete the text.

@ YOUSSEF'S PLACE, MARRAKESH

Last year, we [1]*don't have* / *didn't have* / *didn't had* a holiday here in the UK. We went to Morocco. We [2]*don't stayed* / *weren't stay* / *didn't stay* at a hotel – we camped at 'Youssef's place' near Marrakesh. We had a big tent with two beds. The campsite was very beautiful and there were a lot of great people there. (We [3]*didn't meet* / *didn't met* / *don't met* Youssef, but we met his brother!)

Youssef's place isn't in Marrakesh – it's about 40 minutes from the city. We [4]*not drove* / *didn't drove* / *didn't drive* there – we took a taxi. Marrakesh is an exciting city, but we [5]*didn't go* / *don't went* / *didn't went* there every day. We visited small towns and villages near the campsite and walked in the mountains.

The holiday wasn't expensive. The tent cost $30 a night and we usually cooked our meals in the campsite kitchen. But we [6]*don't cook* / *not cooked* / *didn't cook* every night! We visited some great restaurants and cafés in Marrakesh.

b Complete the conversations with the past simple negative form of the verbs in brackets.

1 **A** Our father went to Los Angeles last week. He stayed at a hotel, I think.
B No, he _didn't stay_ (stay) at a hotel. He stayed at a campsite.

2 **A** We visited a lot of museums on holiday.
B We __________ (visit) a lot of museums. We visited two museums! That's not a lot!

3 **A** How was the café?
B I went to the office! I __________ (go) to a café!

4 **A** They had a car on holiday in France.
B Well, no, they __________ (have) a car. They had bikes.

5 **A** I bought a few new clothes yesterday.
B You __________ (buy) a few new clothes! You bought a lot of new clothes!

6 **A** I read a lot of books last weekend.
B You __________ (read) a lot of books. You read one book! That's all!

c 09.01 Listen and check.

2 VOCABULARY Transport

a Write the words under the pictures.

bike boat bus car metro plane taxi train ~~tram~~

1 _tram_

2 __________

3 __________

4 __________

5 __________

6 __________

7 __________

8 __________

9 __________

3 PRONUNCIATION
Sound and spelling: the letter *a*

a 09.02 Listen to the words in the box. What sound do the **marked** letters have? Complete the table.

~~what~~ taxi car flat train father take plane watch want camp garden

/æ/ (e.g. *cat*)	/ɑː/ (e.g. *park*)	/eɪ/ (e.g. *plate*)	/ɒ/ (e.g. *not*)
			what

9B HOW DID YOU GET THERE?

1 GRAMMAR Past simple: questions

a Put the words in the correct order to make questions.

1 last / did / go / holiday / year / on / where / you ?
Where did you go on holiday last year?
2 you / did / there / how / get ?
____
3 go / friend / a / you / with / did ?
____
4 stay / you / did / where ?
____
5 up / get / what / did / you / time ?
____
6 lot / buy / things / of / you / did / a ?
____
7 did / beach / the / go / you / to ?
____
8 holiday / did / enjoy / you / the ?
____

b Complete the conversation with the words in the box.

Did he	was	~~did~~	did he get	Did Jack stay
Did you	did you stay	he did	he didn't	I didn't

A What [1] *did* you do on New Year's Eve? [2]__________ go out?
B No, [3]__________. I stayed at home.
A Really? Why [4]__________ at home?
B I wasn't very well.
A Oh, no! [5]__________ at home?
B No, [6]__________. He went into the city.
A [7]__________ see the fireworks?
B Yes, [8]__________.
A What time [9]__________ home?
B I don't know. I [10]__________ in bed!

c 09.03 Listen and check.

2 VOCABULARY The seasons and the weather

a Find the four seasons and six weather words.

(r	a	i	n	y)	j	x	l	y	s
z	y	v	p	x	l	z	z	p	p
f	w	a	r	m	j	q	c	k	r
f	y	p	n	b	h	v	o	d	i
y	j	a	q	k	o	x	l	x	n
c	l	u	s	k	t	v	d	d	g
l	b	t	j	z	h	q	t	p	p
o	f	u	q	s	u	m	m	e	r
u	b	m	v	n	k	t	l	v	z
d	q	n	n	j	p	y	f	t	s
y	x	b	v	t	j	z	y	k	n
q	w	i	n	t	e	r	v	q	o
y	p	s	u	n	n	y	z	j	w

b Underline the correct words to complete the conversations.

1 **A** It's –7 °C! I don't like [1]*summer* / *<u>winter</u>*!
B Really? I like this season. I like [2]*cloud* / *cold* weather and I really like [3]*snowy* / *snow*!
2 **A** It's really [4]*wind* / *windy* today.
B Yes, there's always a lot of [5]*wind* / *windy* in the autumn.
3 **A** Look at the [6]*rain* / *rainy*!
B I know. It often [7]*rains* / *rainy* in this country.
4 **A** Did you have good weather on holiday? It was 42°C here.
B 42°C! It wasn't [8]*hot*, / *cold*, but it was [9]*warm* / *wind* and [10]*sun* / *sunny* every day.

c 09.04 Listen and check.

3 PRONUNCIATION Sound and spelling: the letter *o*

a 09.05 Listen to the words in the box. What sound do the **marked** letters have? Complete the table.

~~cl**o**ud~~	h**o**t	sn**o**wy	h**o**liday	t**o**wn	c**o**ld
ph**o**ne	ag**o**	d**o**ctor	br**o**wn	wr**o**ng	tr**o**users

/əʊ/ (e.g., *no*)	/aʊ/ (e.g., *now*)	/ɒ/ (e.g., *not*)
	cloud	

9C EVERYDAY ENGLISH
Can you do something for me?

1 USEFUL LANGUAGE
Making and responding to requests

a Complete the conversations with the sentences in the box.

Sorry, I can't. I'm really busy.
Thanks, that's really kind of you.
Sure, no problem.
Can you do something for me?
Oh, OK, I'll do it then.
Could you meet me at the station on Sunday?
~~Can you go to the shops?~~

Conversation 1

A 1 *Can you go to the shops?* We need bread.
B Sorry, I'm really busy.
A 2 ______

Conversation 2

A 3 ______
B Sure, what is it?
A 4 ______
B Yes, certainly.
A 5 ______

Conversation 3

A Can you come to the shops with me today?
B 6 ______
A Oh, OK. Could you come with me tomorrow?
B 7 ______
A Thanks.

b 09.06 Listen and check.

c Put the conversation in the correct order.

- [ ] **KARINA** Can you pick Jenny up from school at four?
- [1] **KARINA** Hi Saúl.
- [ ] **KARINA** See you later.
- [ ] **KARINA** Thanks, that's really kind of you.
- [ ] **KARINA** I'm fine, thanks. Could you do something for me?
- [ ] **SAÚL** Yes, of course. What is it?
- [ ] **SAÚL** Sure, no problem.
- [ ] **SAÚL** Hi Karina. How are you?
- [ ] **SAÚL** That's OK. See you later.

d 09.07 Listen and check.

2 PRONUNCIATION
Syllables and spelling

a 09.08 Listen to the words in the box. How many syllables do they have? Put the words in the correct column.

~~lovely~~ ~~expensive~~ beautiful station autumn different museum cinema restaurant interesting holiday campsite

2 syllables	3 syllables
lovely	*expensive*

9C SKILLS FOR WRITING

After that, we went to a party

1 READING

a Read three posts online about New Year's Eve and tick (✓) the correct people. Sometimes there is more than one possible answer.

	Jiang	Luke	Fernanda
1 Who had dinner in a restaurant?			✓
2 Who had fish for dinner?			
3 Who wore new clothes?			
4 Who met some friends?			
5 Who was with family?			
6 Who watched TV?			
7 Who cleaned the house?			
8 Who saw fireworks?			

What Did You Do Last New Year's Eve?

First, my sisters and I cleaned the house. Then, we went shopping for new clothes. I bought a red dress for New Year's Eve. After that, we cooked fish, vegetables and rice for dinner. We had a big family New Year's Eve dinner at our home with our parents and grandparents. We didn't go out, but we saw a lot of fireworks near our house.

***Jiang**, China*

Like | Reply | Share

First, I went to my brother's flat and we watched a film. We had pizza and ice cream. It was OK. Then, we went into town and met some friends. It was really cold (I only had my old black jeans and T-shirt – no coat or hat!), but we watched the fireworks for about ten minutes. After that, I went home and watched TV.

***Luke**, UK*

Like | Reply | Share

First, I had dinner in a restaurant with my friends. I had fish and it was very good. After that, we went to a party on the beach. It was great! I wore a new white dress. There were a lot of people on the beach. We put flowers in the water and watched the fireworks. After that, we sat and talked until about 4:00 am.

***Fernanda**, Brazil*

Like | Reply | Share

2 WRITING SKILLS

Making the order clear

a Underline the correct words to complete the online posts.

What Did You Do on Your **Last Birthday?**

I'm a doctor, so I was at work in the day – but the evening was fun! 1 *First that, / First,* my friend Tess arrived at my house with a beautiful birthday cake. 2 *After, / Then,* my friend Daniel phoned from Edinburgh. 3 *After that, / After,* I met my sister at a Chinese restaurant and we had a really good dinner.

Lola 1 like

For my last birthday, I went to London with my friend James. We went on a boat on the river in the morning. It was nice, but it was very cold! 4 *First, / After that,* we had lunch and 5 *next that / then* we went to a football match. Our team didn't win, but we had a good time anyway!

Jon 3 likes

Last year, I had a really fun birthday. 6 *First, / Next,* I had lunch with my family. 7 *After then, / Then,* I went shopping with my sister. I bought some clothes and a nice new watch. 8 *After that, / Next time,* I met my friends Iris, Calvin and Robert. We had dinner and talked all evening.

Sienna 1 like

3 WRITING

a What did you do last New Year's Eve? Write an online post.

UNIT 9
Reading and listening extension

1 READING

a Read the article. Match the people to pictures 1–3.

Harry ☐ Monica ☐ Lucio ☐

b Read the article again. Complete the sentences with *Harry*, *Monica* or *Lucio*.

1 ___Lucio___ travelled with a friend.
2 __________ wanted to surprise a friend.
3 __________ made a journey to find a new job.
4 __________ was on holiday.
5 __________ met an important person on a journey.
6 __________ didn't see his or her friend.
7 __________ had a problem because of the weather.
8 __________ didn't arrive at the correct hotel.

c Write about a journey you took. Remember to give information about:

- when the journey was
- why you went on the journey
- where you travelled from and to
- what happened on the journey.

WE ASKED OUR READERS TO SEND IN THEIR TRAVEL STORIES. HERE ARE SOME OF THEM:

Harry, 35

Four years ago, I went to Bristol for a job interview. Train tickets are expensive in the UK, so I went by bus. The journey was about five hours. I didn't have anything to read so I started talking to the woman in the seat next to me. Her name was Ana. We got married last year and now we have a baby boy!

Monica, 27

I was in Canada on business and I had some free time, so I flew to Vancouver to visit my friend Chloe. I didn't tell her because I wanted to surprise her. I arrived, but Chloe wasn't at home. The man in the flat next door said she was on holiday! I got a taxi back to the airport, but it started to snow. There were no flights, so I slept at the airport. It was awful!

Lucio, 20

For our holiday, my friend and I decided to spend a week at the beach. We found a nice hotel online and paid for our room. It was a long drive and we arrived late at night. Then the receptionist said she didn't have a room for us at the hotel. We were so tired! We went to the beach and slept under the stars. The next morning, we realized we went to the wrong hotel!

2 LISTENING

a 09.09 Listen to the interview. Underline the correct words to complete the sentences.

1 The woman is <u>*working*</u> / *on holiday* today.
2 The woman *knows* / *doesn't know* the man.
3 The man and woman met *on holiday last year* / *in the street today*.
4 They talk about the *man's* / *woman's* holiday.

b 09.09 Listen again. Tick (✓) the sentences that are true. Correct the false sentences.

1 ☐ The man's last holiday was in summer.
The man's last holiday was in autumn.
2 ☐ He went on holiday with his children.
3 ☐ They travelled by ship and train.
4 ☐ They were on holiday for two weeks.
5 ☐ They stayed in a flat near the beach.
6 ☐ It was their first visit to Portugal.
7 ☐ The man learnt some Portuguese phrases before the holiday.
8 ☐ England is often cold and rainy in autumn.

c Write a conversation between two friends talking about their last holiday. Think about these questions:

- Where did they go?
- How did they get there?
- Where did they stay?
- How was the weather?

Review

1 GRAMMAR

Tick (✓) the past simple sentences that are correct. Correct the mistakes.

1 ☐ **A** Did you take these photos?
B Yes, I took.
Yes, I did.
2 ☐ Where did you go?
3 ☐ I didn't saw Azra.
4 ☐ What time you arrived?
5 ☐ Elena didn't get up early.
6 ☐ What did they do?
7 ☐ **A** Did you visit your friends?
B No, I didn't visit.
8 ☐ Matt didn't read his emails.

2 VOCABULARY

Correct the mistakes.

1 The weather's very cold and cloud today.
The weather's very cold and cloudy today.
2 We took train to Milan.
3 We went with plane to Melbourne.
4 This is a photo of the snowy in the garden.
5 **A** Did you drive to the station?
B No, we went by the bus.
6 It always rainy here in the summer.
7 Did you go with car to Málaga?
8 It was suny and warm yesterday.

REVIEW YOUR PROGRESS

Look again at Review Your Progress on p. 78 of the Student's Book. How well can you do these things now?
3 = very well 2 = well 1 = not so well

I CAN ...	
talk about travel and holiday experiences	☐
talk about past holidays	☐
make and respond to requests.	☐

10A WE'RE WATCHING THE MATCH

1 GRAMMAR Present continuous: positive

a Underline the correct words to complete the text messages.

1 *I'm cook* / *I'm cooking* / *I cooking* dinner. There's a lot of food. Do you want to eat?

2 *Jaime listening* / *Jaime's listens* / *Jaime's listening* to a podcast. It's really boring!

3 I'm at the station. *It's raining* / *It raining* / *It's rain* and I don't have an umbrella. Can you pick me up?

4 *We're having* / *We having* / *We're have* coffee in the Peach Tree Café. See you soon.

5 *I looking* / *I'm looking* / *I'm look* out the window and I can see your cat. *It sitting* / *It's sitting* / *It is sit* in a tree!

b Complete the sentences with the present continuous form of the verbs in the box. Use contractions.

go ~~have~~ drink study wear work

1 They 're having dinner.

2 She ______ coffee.

3 We ______ to school.

4 I ______ in the office today.

5 He ______ a white shirt.

6 You ______ at the library.

2 VOCABULARY The home

a Complete the crossword puzzle.

→ Across

3 There's a shower in this room.
4 There's a table and six chairs in this room. We have dinner here every evening. (6, 4)
6 Every room has one or more. It's good to open it in hot weather.
7 There are a lot of nice chairs in this room and a big TV. (6, 4)
8 Every room has one. You walk on it.

↓ Down

1 There's a table and two chairs in this room. I cook and eat here.
2 Every room has one or two. You use it to go in or out.
3 I read books, listen to music, sleep and wake up in this room.
5 We sit here on sunny days but not on rainy days!
6 Every room has four or more. You can put pictures there.

3 PRONUNCIATION Sound and spelling: /tʃ/ and /θ/

a 10.01 Listen to the words in the box. What sound do the **marked** letters have? Complete the table.

~~bathroom~~ kit**ch**en pic**t**ure **ch**air nin**th** mon**th** ques**t**ion **th**irty

/tʃ/ (e.g., *lun**ch***)	/θ/ (e.g., *ba**th***)
	bathroom

10B ARE YOU WORKING?

1 GRAMMAR Present continuous: negative and questions

a Put the words in the correct order to make questions and statements.

1 you / are / who / phoning ?
Who are you phoning?

2 studying / aren't / we .
______

3 phone / is / the / Emir / talking / why / on ?
______

4 not / book / I'm / this / reading .
______

5 are / bus / waiting / for / friends / the / your ?
______

6 the / staying / hotel / isn't / at / Greta .
______

b 10.02 Listen and check.

c Complete the conversation with the present continuous form of the verbs in brackets.

ANDY Hi, it's me. Where are you? What [1] *are you doing* (you / do)?
TILDA I'm with Jenny and Craig.
ANDY Oh, [2] ______ (you / work)?
TILDA Yes, we are. Can I have some apple juice, please?
ANDY Apple juice? What [3] ______ (you / talk) about?
TILDA Sorry, [4] ______ (I / not / talk) to you. [5] ______ (I / talk) to the waiter, but he [6] ______ (not / listen).
ANDY Waiter? Is there a waiter at work?
TILDA No, [7] ______ (we / not / work) in the office. We're in a meeting at a café.
ANDY Oh …

d 10.03 Listen and check.

2 VOCABULARY Place phrases with prepositions

a Complete the sentences with *in*, *on* or *at*.

1 Is Albie *in* bed?
2 Sorry, I can't talk now. I'm ______ the airport.
3 Were you ______ school yesterday?
4 Why did you take photos ______ the plane?
5 Zoe's ______ the bus stop.
6 Kay and Ellie are ______ holiday.
7 Did you read ______ the train?
8 I talked to Jason ______ the party.
9 Your bag is ______ the car.
10 I saw this film ______ the cinema last year.
11 Is there wi-fi ______ the hotel?
12 I have wi-fi ______ home.

b Underline the correct words to complete the conversations.

1 **A** Where are you? Are you *at / in / on* the airport?
B No, I'm *at / in / on* a restaurant with Marco!
2 **A** Is Pasha *at / in / on* work?
B No, he's *at / in / on* holiday.
3 **A** You could phone Isabella. She's *at / in / on* home.
B I don't have my phone. It's *at / in / on* the car.
4 **A** Is Emma *at / in / on* school?
B No, she's *at / in / on* bed.
5 **A** Are you *at / in / on* the bus?
B No, there aren't any buses. I'm *at / in / on* a taxi.
6 **A** I'm still *at / in / on* the station. The train's late.
B Oh dear. Can you text me when you're *at / in / on* the train?

c 10.04 Listen and check.

3 PRONUNCIATION Sound and spelling: /ə/

a 10.05 Listen and underline the /ə/ sound in each word.

1 husband
2 picture
3 Brazil
4 daughter
5 autumn
6 ago
7 Japanese
8 hospital
9 computer
10 afternoon

10C EVERYDAY ENGLISH

What time's the next train to London?

1 USEFUL LANGUAGE
Asking for travel information

a Complete the expressions with the words in the box.

four o'clock office train ~~six~~ stop ten minutes

1 platform _six_
2 ticket ______
3 direct ______
4 in ______
5 at ______
6 bus ______

b Complete the conversation with the words in the box.

at can bus stop direct change
~~excuse~~ help problem next ticket

A Oh [1] _excuse_ me!
B Yes? How [2] ______ I help?
A What time's the [3] ______ bus to Seville?
B It's [4] ______ 11:15.
A So it leaves in ten minutes. Is it a [5] ______ bus?
B No, you [6] ______ at Córdoba.
A OK, and which [7] ______ is it?
B Number 2, near the [8] ______ office.
A Great! Thanks for your [9] ______.
B No [10] ______.

c 10.06 Listen and check.

d Put the conversation in the correct order.

☐ **B** No problem.
☐ **B** Yes? How can I help?
☐ **B** No, you change at Brighton.
1 **A** Excuse me.
☐ **A** What time's the next train to Eastbourne?
☐ **B** The next train leaves in half an hour.
☐ **A** So at 10:25. Is it a direct train?
☐ **B** It's platform 9.
☐ **A** OK, and which platform is it?
☐ **A** Great! Thanks for your help.

e 10.07 Listen and check.

2 PRONUNCIATION
Sound and spelling: /ɪə/ and /eə/

a 10.08 Listen to the words in the box. What sound do the **marked** letters have? Complete the table.

~~p**ai**r~~ w**ea**r w**e're** m**ea**l th**ere**
y**ea**r h**ere** ch**ai**r wh**ere** cl**ea**r

/ɪə/ (e.g., *dear*)	/eə/ (e.g., *hair*)
	pair

10C SKILLS FOR WRITING
What time does it start?

1 READING

a Read the messages. Are the sentences true (*T*) or false (*F*)?

1 Sandy and Eliana are at the cinema.
2 Leo wants information about the film and the cinema.
3 Sian is walking in the rain.
4 Sian needs information about a football match and a concert.
5 Kerem isn't driving to the train station.
6 Kerem has a ticket for the train.

Leo: Hi Sandy! I'm having lunch with Eliana and she'd like to come to the cinema with us tomorrow. Sorry, I can't remember two things. What time does the film start? And which cinema is it? Thanks!

Sian: Hi Oliver. It's a lovely day here today – very cold but sunny. I'm walking to the shops and I want to buy something for Gabriel. Can you tell me two things? Does he like football? And what sort of music does he like? Thanks!

Kerem: Hi Catalina. I'm late for the train, but I'm in a taxi. Two questions: Do you have my train ticket or do I need to buy a ticket? Which platform does the train leave from? See you soon!

2 WRITING SKILLS
Word order in questions

a Complete the questions. Write one word in each gap.

1 **A** How much *were* *the* *tickets*?
B The tickets were £8.50.
2 **A** ______ ______ ______ late?
B Yes, the train's late.
3 **A** He's going home.
B Why ______ ______ ______ home?
4 **A** Where ______ ______ ______ this T-shirt?
B I didn't buy this T-shirt – my brother gave it to me.
5 **A** What time ______ ______ ______ ______?
B The film starts at 4:45 pm.
6 **A** Where ______ I ______ a taxi?
B You can get a taxi outside the station.
7 **A** ______ ______ ______ ______ restaurant?
B Yes, it's an expensive restaurant.
8 **A** ______ ______ ______ ______ a car park?
B Yes, the hotel has a car park.

b Put the words in the correct order to make questions.

1 from / you / are / where ?
Where are you from?
2 on / Nick / playing / the / computer / is ?
______
3 have / their / how / does / flat / rooms / many ?
______
4 the / yesterday / give / any / did / teacher / homework / us ?
______
5 can / where / ticket / a / bus / buy / I ?
______
6 he / school / today / at / was ?
______

3 WRITING

a Write a message to another student and ask for information about your new English class. Ask about:

- the classroom
- the time of the class
- the homework.

UNIT 10
Reading and listening extension

1 READING

a Read the email. Tick (✓) the sentences that are true. Correct the false sentences.

1 ☐ Josie is on holiday in Italy.
Josie is on holiday in Turkey.

2 ☐ Ava is studying Italian.

3 ☐ There are three people in the Italian family.

4 ☐ Today is Saturday.

5 ☐ Ava is in her bedroom at the moment.

6 ☐ Most people in the family are outside now.

7 ☐ Ava wants to know what Marco is doing.

80%

Reply Forward

Hi Josie,

Thanks for your email. I hope you're enjoying your holiday in Turkey. I'm in Milan in Italy for two weeks. Mum and Dad sent me here to do an Italian course. I didn't really want to come!

I'm staying with an Italian family here. The parents are Marco and Rosa, and they have two sons, Andrea and Georgio. Andrea is 17 and Georgio is 14. They're very friendly, but they only speak Italian, and sometimes I don't understand them.

It's Sunday, and everyone is at home, but we're all in different parts of the house. I'm writing this email in my bedroom. It's really nice because I can see the garden from my window. Andrea is in the garden. It's raining, but he's playing with the dog. Georgio is in the room next to me. His parents think he is studying for his exams, but he's playing a video game and texting his friends.

Rosa is in the living room. She's a teacher and she's preparing her lessons for next week. Marco is cooking dinner and listening to some terrible opera music. I don't know what he's making, but he's a great cook. My dad can only make toast!

Anyway, what are you doing? Write and let me know.

Ava

b Read the email again. Underline the correct words to complete the sentences.

1 *Josie* / *Ava* / *Ava's parents* organised Ava's trip to Milan.
2 It's a *one-week* / *two-week* / *three-week* course.
3 Ava is staying in *a hotel* / *a house* / *a flat* in Italy.
4 Ava doesn't always *hear* / *understand* / *listen to* what the family members say to her.
5 *Marco* / *Georgio* / *Andrea* isn't inside the house right now.
6 Georgio is *studying* / *playing a game* / *texting his parents*.
7 Rosa is *relaxing* / *working* / *helping Marco*.
8 Ava doesn't like Marco's *children* / *food* / *music*.

c Write a description of an evening in your home. Remember to give information about:

- who is in your home
- where each person is
- what each person is doing.

2 LISTENING

a 10.09 Listen. Complete the sentences with the names in the box.

~~Jack~~ Mum Melinda Dad Tim

1 Jack is at home.
2 ________ is at work.
3 ________ is at the sports centre.
4 ________ and ________ are at the train station.

b 10.09 Listen again. Underline the correct words to complete the sentences.

1 Jack's dad is *working in* / *calling* his office.
2 Jack is *at home* / *at the movies*.
3 Jack is *watching TV* / *listening to music*.
4 Melinda and her friends *are* / *aren't* at Melinda's house.
5 Jack's mum is with *her husband* / *one of her sons*.
6 Tim's not wearing a *coat* / *jumper*.
7 It's starting to *snow* / *rain*.
8 The station *is* / *isn't* busy.

c You are somewhere in your home town. Write a phone conversation between you and a friend. Remember to say:

- where you are
- what you are doing
- what is happening around you.

Review

1 GRAMMAR

Correct the mistakes.

1 I driving to the hospital.
I'm driving to the hospital.
2 She don't working today.
3 You having lunch?
4 Where Elena going?
5 They're siting in the garden.
6 It raining?
7 No, it not.
8 Yes, is.

2 VOCABULARY

Tick (✓) the sentences that are correct. Correct the mistakes.

1 ☐ Is Sofía in the livving room?
Is Sofía in the living room?
2 ☐ Cara's on holiday.
3 ☐ I'm in the kitchin.
4 ☐ Gaby's at home.
5 ☐ Amber's on the bus.
6 ☐ They're in the dinning room.
7 ☐ She's at a party.
8 ☐ Jorge isn't at bed.
9 ☐ I'm at airport.
10 ☐ We're on a taxi.

REVIEW YOUR PROGRESS

Look again at Review Your Progress on p. 86 of the Student's Book. How well can you do these things now?
3 = very well 2 = well 1 = not so well

I CAN ...	
talk about my home	☐
ask where people are and what they're doing	☐
ask for travel information.	☐

11A SHE WENT AROUND THE EARTH

1 GRAMMAR Object pronouns

a Underline the correct words.

1 Where are the tickets? I had *they* / *them* a minute ago.
2 *We* / *Us* like Theo a lot. He's staying with *we* / *us* this week.
3 This is my sister. *Me* / *I* phone *her* / *she* every day.
4 I was on TV. Did you see *I* / *me*?
5 Where's my umbrella? I need *her* / *it*!
6 That man's playing tennis really well. *Him* / *He* is really good. Look at *him* / *he*!
7 **A** Bye, John! Bye, Eva! See *you* / *them* tomorrow!
B Bye!

b Complete the conversation with subject and object pronouns.

A [1] ___I___'ve got some photos of the party. [2] _______'re very funny.
B Oh, can I see [3] _______?
A Yes, just a minute … OK … My brother's in this picture. [4] _______ arrived really late.
B Really? Where is [5] _______? I can't see [6] _______!
A [7] _______'s there, with the blue hat!
B Oh yes! [8] _______'s a very big hat! Is that [9] _______? It's your T-shirt.
A Yes, that's [10] _______. I'm with Ian and Debbie. [11] _______'re really nice.
B And who's that?
A That's Anna-Maria. [12] _______'s at our house now. [13] _______'s staying with [14] _______.
B Can I meet [15] _______?
A Yes, of course. [16] _______ really wants to meet [17] _______!

c 11.01 Listen and check.

2 VOCABULARY Life events

a Write the words under the pictures.

be born die go to school finish university ~~get married~~
go to university grow up have a baby stop working

1 get married

2 _______

3 _______

4 _______

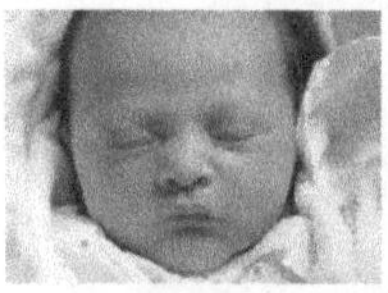
5 _______

6 _______

7 _______

8 _______

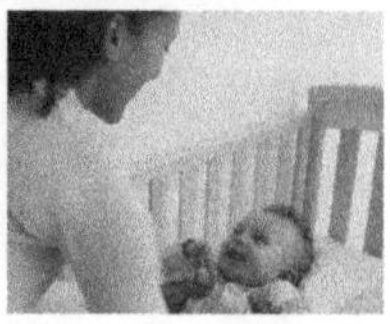
9 _______

b Underline the correct words to complete the text.

Liliana, Rosa and Me

Liliana [1] *was* / *is* born on 1 January, 1960 in a small town in Colombia. Her family didn't have much money, but they were very happy. Liliana [2] *got to* / *went to* school until she was 16. Then she got a job in an office. She met her husband, Andreas, there. They [3] *got* / *had* a baby girl and they called her Rosa.

Time passed and Rosa grew [4] *on* / *up*. She finished [5] *the school* / *school* and went to [6] *the university* / *university* in the USA. She often visited her parents, but she didn't live with them again. Then sadly, Andreas [7] *stopped* / *died*. He was only 46. Liliana was very sad and she [8] *ended* / *stopped* working.

Three years ago, Liliana came to the USA to be with her daughter, Rosa. I started a conversation with Liliana on a train one day and two weeks later I met Rosa. Rosa and I [9] *got* / *went* married in June!

3 PRONUNCIATION Sound and spelling: /ɜː/

a 11.02 Listen and underline the word which DOESN'T have the /ɜː/ sound.

1	work	sport	shirt
2	daughter	thirty	Thursday
3	university	early	near
4	born	first	world
5	people	person	girl
6	Turkish	grow	weren't

11B SHE CAN PULL A PLANE

1 GRAMMAR *can* for ability

a Underline the correct words to complete the sentences and questions.

1 Your pictures are beautiful! You *can* / *can't* paint very well.
2 **A** *You can* / *Can you* cook?
B Yes, *can I* / *I can*.
3 I like music, but I *can't* / *can* sing at all. I'm a terrible singer!
4 Jenny *can to* / *can* speak Spanish very well.
5 **A** *Can he* / *Cans he* run 10 km?
B No, he *can't* / *doesn't*.
6 They're good swimmers. They *can swim very well* / *can very well swim*.

b 11.03 Listen and check.

c Complete the sentences with *can* or *can't* and a verb in the box.

drive play read say ~~speak~~ swim teach write

1 James can speak Italian quite well.
2 He goes to the beach every day, but he never goes in the water because he ________.
3 Their daughter is only four, but she ________ books.
4 ________ you ________ a car?
5 I like children, but I ________ them. I'm not a teacher.
6 Listen to this! We ________ 'Hello' in Chinese.
7 Look at this! I ________ 'Hello' in Turkish.
8 I'd like to have guitar lessons. I often listen to guitar music, but I ________ the guitar at all.

2 VOCABULARY Abilities

a Match 1–8 to a–h to make questions.

1 [f] Can you ride		a in the sea in your country?
2 [ ] When did you last paint		b dance?
3 [ ] How often do you cook		c a meal for a lot of people?
4 [ ] You're at a party and you like the music. Do you		d 5 km?
5 [ ] Did you sing		e a picture?
6 [ ] Can you run		f a horse?
7 [ ] Do people swim		g a song yesterday?
8 [ ] How often do you drive		h a car?

b 11.04 Listen and check.

c Complete the crossword puzzle with past simple verbs.

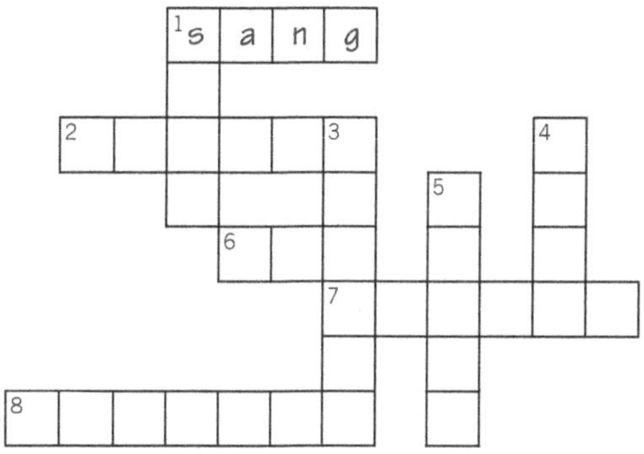

→ Across
1 In the evening, we sat outside and sang ________ songs.
2 I p________ basketball every day when I was in high school.
6 We r________ 5 km in the park this morning.
7 Ellie c________ dinner yesterday. It was very good.
8 Gino p________ a picture of the flowers in the garden.

↓ Down
1 I only s________ for five minutes because the water was very cold!
3 The music was really good and we d________ all night.
4 Noah r________ his bicycle to school every day last week.
5 I d________ our new car for the first time yesterday.

3 PRONUNCIATION *can* / *can't*

a 11.05 Listen to the sentences. Which words are stressed? Tick (✓) the correct box.

1 a [ ] I can swim.
b [✓] I can swim.
2 a [ ] Can you drive?
b [ ] Can you drive?
3 a [ ] Yes, I can.
b [ ] Yes, I can.
4 a [ ] Jim can't sing.
b [ ] Jim can't sing.
5 a [ ] Can he dance?
b [ ] Can he dance?
6 a [ ] No, he can't.
b [ ] No, he can't.

11C EVERYDAY ENGLISH
What do you think?

1 USEFUL LANGUAGE
Talking about opinions

a Complete the sentences and questions with the words in the box.

idea agree right nice ~~so~~ think

1 I don't think ___so___.
2 Maybe you're ___________.
3 I don't think it's a good ___________.
4 I think it's really ___________.
5 What do you ___________?
6 Yes, I ___________.

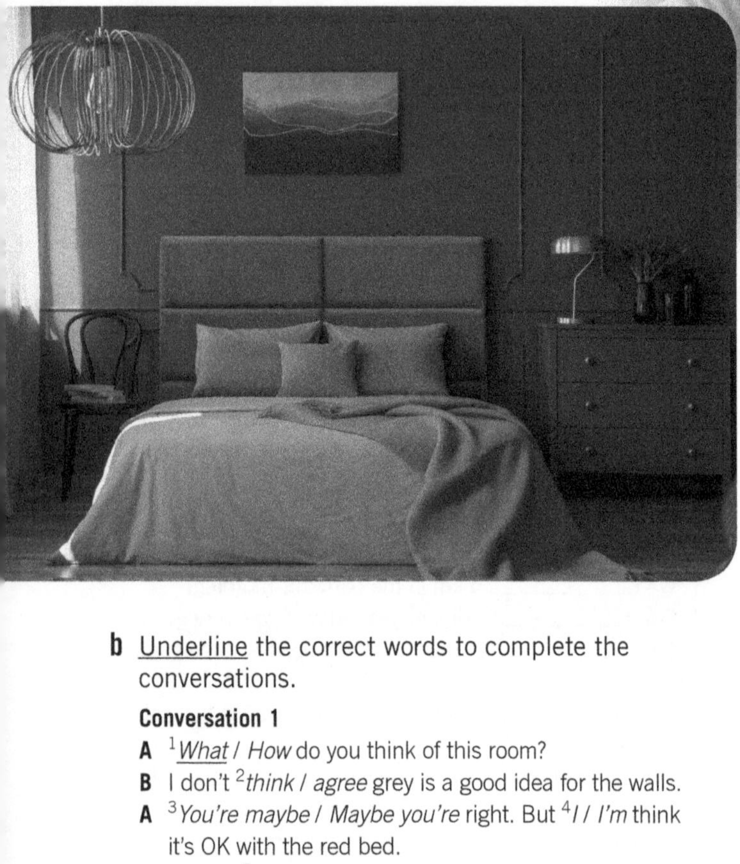

b Underline the correct words to complete the conversations.

Conversation 1

A [1]*What / How* do you think of this room?
B I don't [2]*think / agree* grey is a good idea for the walls.
A [3]*You're maybe / Maybe you're* right. But [4]*I / I'm* think it's OK with the red bed.
B I'm not [5]*so / right* sure.

Conversation 2

A What [6]*are / did* you think of the film?
B It was terrible!
C Yes, [7]*I agree / I'm agree.* It's a really bad film!
A Really? I don't [8]*think so / think.* I liked it.

c 11.06 Listen and check.

d Complete the conversation with one word in each gap. (A contraction, e.g. *I'm* = one word.)

MATEO What do you [1] ___think___ of my new car?
CARMEN I [2] ___________ it's really nice.
PHILIP I'm not [3] ___________ sure.
CARMEN Why not?
PHILIP I [4] ___________ think yellow is a very good colour.
MATEO Maybe you're [5] ___________.
PHILIP Mm.
MATEO What [6] ___________ you think of my old car?

e 11.07 Listen and check.

2 PRONUNCIATION Consonant clusters

a 11.08 Listen and complete the words with the missing letters.

1 touri s t	s t ay
2 e _ _ ineer	e _ _ oy
3 an _ _ er	da _ _ e
4 _ _ _ ool	a _ _
5 thi _ _	ba _ _
6 liste _ _ _	fi _ _
7 clo _ _ _	si _
8 i _ _ eresting	pai _ _

11C SKILLS FOR WRITING

It's a fantastic city

1 READING

a Read the email. Tick (✓) the correct answers.

1 What's Yaz doing in Buenos Aires?
- a ☐ She's working and studying.
- b ☑ She's studying.
- c ☐ She's working.

2 What does Yaz think of Buenos Aires?
- a ☐ She likes it, but she thinks it's expensive.
- b ☐ She doesn't like it.
- c ☐ She likes it because it isn't expensive.

3 Why is Yaz in Buenos Aires?
- a ☐ She's learning to play volleyball.
- b ☐ She's learning to dance.
- c ☐ She's studying IT.

4 What can Santiago do?
- a ☐ He can speak other languages.
- b ☐ He can dance.
- c ☐ He can speak other languages and dance.

5 Where did Yaz and Annette meet?
- a ☐ They met in a bookshop.
- b ☐ They met at a volleyball match.
- c ☐ They met in an IT class.

6 How is Yaz feeling?
- a ☐ She's happy because she isn't at home.
- b ☐ She's having a good time, but she misses people at home.
- c ☐ She's very sad because she misses her friends and family.

Hi Samuel,

Thanks for your email. It was good to hear from you.

I started university here in Buenos Aires six weeks ago and it's going really well. The university's fantastic and Buenos Aires is an exciting city. It's also an expensive city. I'd like to find a job in a shop next year because I really need some money!

As you know, I'm studying IT. It's a really interesting course and the teachers are good. There's a lot of work to do, but there are also a lot of things to do in my free time. I'm learning to dance and I can now play volleyball quite well.

I'm making some new friends here. Santiago and Annette are really nice. I met Santiago at my dance class. He's a language student and he can speak Spanish, Italian and German very well. He's also a good dancer and he helps me in the lessons. Annette is studying IT and we met in the university bookshop on the first day. We often study together in the evening.

The people here are really nice, but I miss my family at home. I miss my friends, too. Write again soon!

Best wishes,

Yaz

2 WRITING SKILLS Pronouns

a Read the email. Change the words in brackets to subject and object pronouns.

Hi Freya,

Thank you very much for your long emails! I read 1 _them_ (*your long emails*) in a café every morning. I like the photos, too. 2 ____________ (*The photos*) are very funny!

Things here in Rome are going well. 3 ____________ (*Rome's*) a big city with a lot of beautiful places to visit. I study at a language school called Accademia Leonardo. 4 ____________ (*Accademia Leonardo's*) a really big school, but the classes are small and the teachers are great. My teacher is called Viola. 5 ____________ (*Viola's*) a really good teacher and I like 6 ____________ (*Viola*) very much.

I have a new friend called Luigi. He's from Venice. I met 7 ____________ (*Luigi*) at a museum! We started talking about the pictures and then 8 ____________ (*Luigi and I*) went out for coffee together.

How are you? Do you see Jess and Otto? I miss 9 ____________ (*Jess and Otto*) a lot. And I miss 10 ____________ (*Freya*) too, of course!

Write again soon,

Abby

3 WRITING

a Write an email to a friend. Give information about:

- where you are now
- where you study English
- your teacher
- the other students in your class
- what you do in the evening.

Hi ____________,

____

____

____

____

____

____

____

____

____

____

____

____

UNIT 11
Reading and listening extension

1 READING

a Read the TV review. Tick (✓) the parts of Elsa's life you read about.

1 her family ✓
2 her house ☐
3 her school ☐
4 her work ☐
5 her interests ☐
6 her husband's work ☐
7 the death of her husband ☐
8 her children ☐
9 her friends ☐

b Read the review again. Put the events in Elsa's life in the order they happened.

☐ Her husband died.
☐ She had a baby.
☐ She went to South Africa.
☐ She finished university.
☐ She started teaching.
☐ She got married.
1 She left Dundee.
☐ She got a job in Edinburgh.

c Choose an interesting member of your family and write about his or her life. Remember to give information about:

- where and when the person was born
- where the person lived
- what work the person did
- the person's family
- why the person was interesting.

LAST NIGHT'S TV

People's Lives is a popular TV programme on Channel 12. The programme helps people find out about their family history.

Last night, the programme was about Olivia Noon and her grandmother, Elsa. Olivia didn't know her grandmother well because Elsa died when Olivia was two years old. *People's Lives* found out that Elsa was from Dundee in Scotland. She was born there in 1922 and had six brothers and sisters. The family was poor and Elsa went to Edinburgh when she was 17. She got a job in a hospital there.

Elsa worked at the hospital for six years. Then she studied at university to be a doctor. She was 32 when she finished university and 33 when she married Olivia's grandfather, James. James was a businessman from Cambridge.

Elsa and James were very happy for three years and they had a son, but then James died.

Elsa left Scotland and went to South Africa on a ship with her son. She worked as a doctor there and started a hospital for women. In 1972, Elsa returned to Dundee to teach at a university there. She taught students who wanted to be doctors. Elsa died in Dundee in 1984.

It was an interesting programme and Olivia was very happy to know more about her grandmother. Next week, it is George Freeman's turn to find out about his grandparents. Don't forget to watch!

- ***People's Lives*, 8 pm next Wednesday, Channel 12**

2 LISTENING

a 11.09 Listen to the conversation. Put the jobs in the order that you hear them.

- ☐ chef
- ☐ English teacher
- ☐ receptionist
- [1] singer
- ☐ tour guide

b 11.09 Listen again. Tick (✓) the things that Camila can do.

1 sing	☐
2 cook	✓
3 swim	☐
4 speak a foreign language	☐
5 teach	☐
6 speak English	☐
7 drive	☐

c 11.09 Listen again. Underline the correct words.

1 Alex and Camila are *<u>at work</u>* / *at home.*
2 Camila works in *a shop* / *an office* now.
3 *Alex* / *Camila* wants to find a new job.
4 Alex mentions *one job* / *two jobs* on a ship.
5 Camila speaks English and *French* / *Spanish.*
6 Camila doesn't want to live in a very *hot* / *cold* country.
7 Camila *knows* / *doesn't know* a lot about York.
8 Camila decides to apply for the job in *Manchester* / *York.*

d Write a conversation between two friends. One person describes a job he or she would like to do. The other person asks questions. Remember to say:

- what the job is
- why he or she wants to do this job
- why he or she is a good person for this job.

Review

1 GRAMMAR

Correct the mistakes.

1 I have some eggs. We can have it for breakfast.
I have some eggs. We can have them for breakfast.
2 Your dad's an engineer. We could ask her for help.
3 Is your phone new? I like him.
4 Your sister's really nice. How often do you see them?
5 He can to ride a horse.
6 You can drive?
7 I not can sing.
8 **A** Can they swim?
B Yes, they swim.

2 VOCABULARY

Correct the mistakes.

1 Anita and Jacob had baby in March.
Anita and Jacob had a baby in March.
2 I born in 1999.
3 She was died in 2012.
4 I finished at university last year.
5 I grew in a small town in Ecuador.
6 My father stopped to work last year.
7 She singed a song last week.
8 I rode the car to the station.
9 I run 10 km last Saturday.
10 We swim in the new swimming pool yesterday.

REVIEW YOUR PROGRESS

Look again at Review Your Progress on p. 94 of the Student's Book. How well can you do these things now?
3 = very well 2 = well 1 = not so well

I CAN ...	
talk about people's lives	☐
talk about things I know how to do	☐
talk about opinions.	☐

12A I'M GOING TO HAVE A LONG HOT BATH

1 GRAMMAR
be going to: positive and negative

a Underline the correct words to complete the conversations.

Conversation 1

A Is there an email from Stephen? [1] *He going to* / *He's going to* / *He's going* write to you with information about the boat trip.

B I don't know. [2] *I'm going not to* / *I'm not going to* / *I'm not going* check my emails today or tomorrow.

A Oh, OK. Well, I'm going [3] *to phone* / *phoning* / *phone* him this evening, so I can ask him then.

Conversation 2

A It's the holidays! [4] *I go to* / *I'm going* / *I'm going to* sleep for ten hours every night! [5] *I going* / *I'm going* / *I'm go* to watch TV every day!

B Really? That's so boring! My brother and I [6] *am going* / *is going* / *are going* to work on a farm near the mountains. The people there [7] *are going* / *is going* / *am going* to teach us how to ride horses.

A Hmm, sounds quite interesting. What about your sister?

B [8] *She's going not* / *She not going* / *She isn't going* to come with us. She wants to stay at home.

b 12.01 Listen and check.

c Complete the sentences with the *be going to* form of the verbs in the box.

cook do have ~~play~~ (not) ride (not) sing (not) stay (not) use watch

1 We __are going to play__ volleyball tomorrow.
2 My sister ________ dinner for me this evening.
3 I ________ a song!
4 Samantha ________ yoga this afternoon.
5 They ________ at expensive hotels.
6 Luis ________ his motorbike fast.
7 I ________ a long, hot bath.
8 We ________ a film on TV this evening.
9 You ________ your phone in the restaurant!

2 VOCABULARY
Months and future time expressions

a Tick (✓) the correct ending for the sentences.

1 They're going to get married …
a ☐ on June. b ☐ June. c ☑ in June.
2 It's Juan's birthday …
a ☐ in Friday. b ☐ this Friday. c ☐ at Friday.
3 I have a test …
a ☐ at Wednesday. b ☐ next Wednesday. c ☐ in Wednesday.
4 See you …
a ☐ in Monday. b ☐ at Monday. c ☐ on Monday.
5 Can you phone me …
a ☐ this afternoon? b ☐ on afternoon? c ☐ next afternoon?
6 He's going to finish school …
a ☐ in three weeks. b ☐ this three weeks. c ☐ on three weeks.
7 See you …
a ☐ on tomorrow. b ☐ tomorrow. c ☐ in tomorrow.
8 We're going to visit Alia and Ahmed …
a ☐ at the weekend. b ☐ in the weekend. c ☐ the weekend.
9 See you …
a ☐ at the autumn! b ☐ on the autumn! c ☐ in the autumn!
10 She's going to stop working …
a ☐ in month. b ☐ at month. c ☐ next month.

3 VOCABULARY Ordinal numbers

a 12.02 Listen and write the ordinal numbers.

1st	__first__	5th	________	16th	________
2nd	________	9th	________	20th	________
3rd	________	12th	________	22nd	________
4th	________	13th	________	31st	________

4 PRONUNCIATION
Sentence stress: *be going to*

a 12.03 Listen and underline the stressed words in the sentences.

1 You're going to stay at a hotel.
2 They're going to live in Canada.
3 Anna's going to do her homework.
4 I'm going to check my emails.
5 He's going to listen to music.
6 I'm going to read a book.

12B WHAT ARE YOU GOING TO DO THIS WEEKEND?

1 GRAMMAR *be going to*: questions

a Put the words in the correct order to make questions.

1 coffee / to / meet / when / are / we / going / for ?
When are we going to meet for coffee?
2 at / lunch / to / is / going / home / have / he ?
______
3 where / married / to / get / going / they / are ?
______
4 you / station / to / to / are / the / drive / tomorrow / going ?
______
5 to / do / she / evening / going / this / what's ?
______
6 going / potatoes / you / how / are / cook / to / the ?
______

b 12.04 Listen and check.

c Complete the sentences with the *be going to* form of the verbs in brackets.

1 **A** What are you going to do (you / do) this morning?
B I ______ (clean) the house – and you ______ (help) me!
2 **A** So, ______ (he / play) the piano this evening?
B Yes, he is. ______ (you / listen)?
3 **A** What ______ (you and your friends / do) in the holidays?
B I don't know. We ______ (talk) about it this afternoon.
4 **A** Where ______ (she / watch) TV?
B In the living room.
5 When ______ (I / do) all these things on my list?

d 12.05 Listen and check.

2 VOCABULARY Common verbs and collocations

a Match 1–8 with a–h to make sentences.

1 [h] I'm going to make
2 [ ] I'm not going to do
3 [ ] I want to clean
4 [ ] I'd like to paint
5 [ ] We can go
6 [ ] I don't use
7 [ ] I'm going to visit
8 [ ] We're going to invite Alex

a my homework today.
b shopping tomorrow.
c Violet in hospital.
d a picture of you.
e the car. It's really dirty.
f to the party.
g my phone every day.
h a cake for my mum.

b Complete the crossword puzzle.

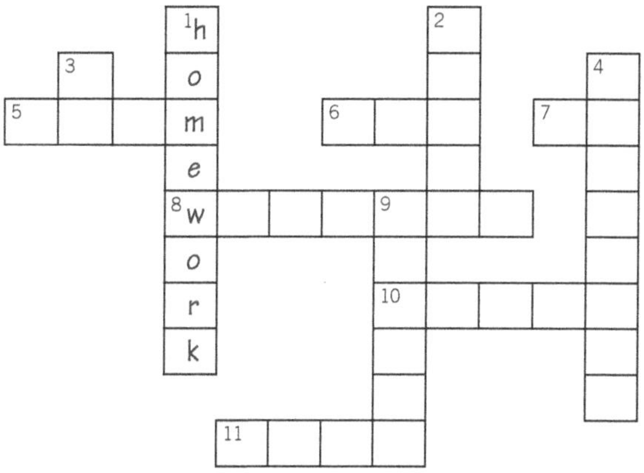

→ Across
5 I didn't paint my r______. I just cleaned it.
6 I need to u______ the Internet.
7 I'd like to g______ for a walk this afternoon.
8 Where are your dirty clothes? I'm going to do the w______.
10 They went to the UK but they didn't v______ London.
11 I'm going to m______ some coffee. Would you like some?

↓ Down
1 I did my homework this morning – English, Maths and Spanish.
2 I'm going to c______ the flat today. It's very dirty. I need a lot of hot water!
3 I d______ sport every day. My favourite sports are tennis and swimming.
4 I use the c______ every day – for email, for work and for music.
9 I'm going to i______ Pedro to my flat to play video games.

3 PRONUNCIATION Sound and spelling: /v/ and /w/

a 12.06 Listen to the words in the box. Do they have the /v/ sound or the /w/ sound? Complete the table.

~~wall~~ evening wi-fi visit November volleyball warm drive windy winter weekend invite

/v/	/w/
	wall

12C EVERYDAY ENGLISH

Would you like to come for dinner?

1 USEFUL LANGUAGE
Making and accepting invitations

a Put the conversation in the correct order.

☐ **B** Yes, I am.
☐ **B** Yes, I'd love to. Thank you.
☐ **B** I'd love to, but I have lots of homework for tomorrow.
☐ **A** Would you like to go to the cinema?
☐ **A** You're a good student! Are you free tomorrow night?
1 **A** Would you like to go to a concert this evening?

b 12.07 Listen and check.

c Put the conversation in the correct order.

1 **A** Would you like to come for dinner tomorrow night?
☐ **A** Great! You can come on Saturday.
☐ **A** Are you free on Friday?
☐ **B** No, sorry. I'm busy on Friday, too. But Saturday's OK.
☐ **B** Thank you!
☐ **B** Sorry, I'm busy then.

d 12.08 Listen and check.

e Complete the conversations with the words in the box.

can come would free busy
~~like~~ thank OK love to

Conversation 1

A Would you [1] ___like___ to come to my party on Saturday?
B I'd [2] __________ to come. Thank you.

Conversation 2

A [3] __________ you like to go to the cinema on Thursday?
B Sorry, I'm [4] __________ then. But Friday's [5] __________.
A OK, we [6] __________ go on Friday.
B Great!

Conversation 3

A Would you like to [7] __________ for lunch at the weekend?
B I'd love [8] __________, but I'm away this weekend.
A Are you [9] __________ next weekend?
B Yes, I am.
A You can come then!
B [10] __________ you. I'd love to come.

f 12.09 Listen and check.

2 PRONUNCIATION
Sound and spelling: *oo*

a 12.10 Listen to the words in the box. What sound do the letters *oo* have? Complete the table.

~~book~~ pool good school food
boots cook look afternoon

/uː/ (e.g., *soon*)	/ʊ/ (e.g., *foot*)
	book

12C SKILLS FOR WRITING

I'm free next weekend

1 READING

a Read the invitations and replies. Are the sentences true (*T*) or false (*F*)?

1 Ed and Hugo are going to have pizza together this evening.
2 Ed is going to make the pizza.
3 They're going to speak on the phone at 2:30 this afternoon.
4 Hugo is free at 7:30 this evening.
5 Nina wants to go shopping in town on Tuesday morning.
6 Selena and Nina are going to meet this Tuesday.
7 Selena can go to Nina's flat this Wednesday.
8 Selena can go to Nina's flat next Wednesday.

Hi Hugo!

How are you? Would you like to meet for dinner today – at about 6:30? There's a new pizza place near the station. People say it's very good. I can call you this afternoon – at about 2:30. Is that OK with you?

Speak later!

Ed

Hi Ed,

I'm good, thanks. I'd love to go for a pizza, but I'm busy at 6:30. Is 7:30 OK for you? I'm going to be at work this afternoon, but we could speak at about 5:30.

Hugo

Hi Selena,

Would you like to come to my flat on Tuesday morning? We could do some online clothes shopping together and I can make lunch.

Best wishes

Nina

Hi Nina,

That's a lovely idea, but I'm staying with friends this week and I'm away until Friday. Maybe we could do it next Tuesday? I'm free next Wednesday, too.

Selena

2 WRITING SKILLS Paragraphs

a Put the text in the correct order to make Henry's email invitation.

☐ Finn's staying with me this week and he can play the guitar really well. We could eat and then sing songs. What do you think? Are you free on Saturday?
☐ I hope you can come!
☐ Hi Juan,
☐ I'm thinking about having a barbecue in the garden on Saturday evening – chicken, fish, vegetables, things like that. Would you and Ada like to come?
☐ Henry

b Put the text in the correct order to make Juan's reply to Henry's email invitation.

☐ Is 8:00 OK? Would you like us to bring some food?
☐ Juan
☐ See you on Saturday!
☐ Thank you, that would be lovely. We're busy on Saturday afternoon, but we can come in the evening.
☐ Hi Henry,

3 WRITING

a Write a reply to the invitation.

Hi!

How are you? I'm going to the beach in my new car this Saturday. Would you like to come with me? We can swim, sit in the sun and play volleyball.

We could go in the morning or the afternoon. What do you think? Maybe Noah and Ben would like to come, too.

Hector

Hi Hector,

____

____

____

____

____

____

____

____

____

____

____

UNIT 12
Reading and listening extension

NEW YEAR, NEW ME
by Matt Simpson

1 Today is January 1st – a good day to start my new life! Some people talk about changing their lives, but they don't do anything. I'm not going to talk about changing my life. I have a list of things I want to do and I'm going to do all of them.

2 What am I going to do first? Well, I usually get up, go to work, come home, have dinner and then watch TV until it's time to go to bed. I never do any sport. From tomorrow, I'm going to get up early every day and go for a run. I'm also going to use the swimming pool at the gym after work.

3 I'm not going to stay at home every evening. I'm going to visit the college to get some information about language courses. I'm interested in Spanish. I also want to do a cookery class. I don't know how to cook, so I usually eat at restaurants or buy pizza. At the weekend, I go to my mum's house for meals!

4 I spend a lot of money on clothes, but I'm not going to buy any more. I'm going to put the money in the bank. My brother and I want to travel and see new places. We're planning to leave our jobs in September and travel around the world.

5 Those are my plans. What are YOU going to do to change your life this year?

1 READING

a Read the blog. Match the ideas a–e to paragraphs 1–5.

a ☐ Travelling to new places
b ☐ Asking about another person's plans
c ☐ Learning new things
d ☐ Deciding to change
e ☐ Changing a daily routine

b Read the blog again. Tick (✓) the activities Matt is going to do.

1 buy more clothes ☐
2 cook a meal for his mum ☐
3 do a lot of travelling ☐
4 get a new job ☐
5 use the gym ☑
6 learn to swim ☐
7 learn to cook ☐
8 play football at the gym ☐
9 run every day ☐
10 save money ☐
11 study a foreign language ☐
12 walk to work every day ☐

c Imagine it's a new year and you want to change your life. Make a list of things you're going to do and things you aren't going to do.

I'm going to ...	I'm not going to ...

2 LISTENING

a 12.11 Listen to the video call. Match the activities in the box with the people. Complete the notes.

have dinner meet friends play tennis read a book see an American football game go to the cinema spend a day at Disneyland take the dog for a walk ~~visit a film studio~~

Marta
visit a film studio
____
____

Lucas
____
____
____

Mum
____
____

Dad
____

b 12.11 Listen again. Are the sentences true (*T*) or false (*F*)?

1 Marta and Lucas are brother and sister.
2 Marta is in the USA.
3 She is travelling around by train.
4 She was in San Francisco yesterday.
5 Rodeo Drive is famous for its shops.
6 The American football game is on Thursday.
7 The next place Marta plans to visit is Las Vegas.
8 Marta is going to phone her parents at the weekend.

c Write a conversation between two friends. One person is going to visit a big city. The other person asks about his or her plans. Remember to say:

- which city he or she's going to visit
- how he or she's going to travel
- what he or she's going to do and see there.

Review

1 GRAMMAR

Tick (✓) the sentences that are correct. Correct the mistakes.

1 ☑ Eduardo isn't going to sleep here tonight. He's at a hotel.
2 ☐ They're going play volleyball. Do you want to watch them?
3 ☐ Are you going to have a bath?
4 ☐ What we are going to do now?
5 ☐ **A** Is he going to work in a bank?
B Yes, he's going.
6 ☐ **A** Is she going to go to university?
B No, she isn't.
7 ☐ I'm going not to get up early. I'm going to stay in bed until lunchtime!
8 ☐ When I going to see you again?

2 VOCABULARY

Correct the mistakes.

1 See you on the two of March.
See you on the second of March.
2 They're going to visit João on the summer.
3 It's the twelve of August.
4 I'm going to start work in Monday.
5 He was born on the fifteenth of Februry.
6 I have bread and cheese. I'm going to do a sandwich.
7 We could visit Lia and Emily to the party. They love parties!
8 I don't really like sport, but I use for a walk every day.
9 I want to clean the walls green.
10 Can I do the computer for five minutes? I need to check my emails.

REVIEW YOUR PROGRESS

Look again at Review Your Progress on p. 102 of the Student's Book. How well can you do these things now?
3 = very well 2 = well 1 = not so well

I CAN ...	
talk about future plans	☐
ask and answer about future plans	☐
make and accept invitations.	☐

VOX POP VIDEO

UNIT 1: Hello!

1a Hello, my name's Marie. What's your name?

a Watch video 1a and underline the correct words.

1 *I'm* / *My name's* Anna.
2 *I'm* / *My name is* Euan.
3 *I'm* / *My name is* Nino.
4 *I'm* / *My name is* Matt.
5 *I'm* / *My name's* Maibritt.
6 *I'm* / *My name's* Samantha.
7 *I'm* / *My name's* Ruby.
8 *I'm* / *My name's* Colin.
9 *I'm* / *My name's* Jo.
10 *I'm* / *My name is* Laurence.
11 *I'm* / *My name's* Sarah.
12 *I'm* / *My name's* Jason.
13 *I'm* / *My name is* Sarah.
14 *I'm* / *My name's* Laura.
15 *I'm* / *My name's* Mark.
16 *I'm* / *My name's* Jenna.
17 *I'm* / *My name's* Claire.
18 *I'm* / *My name's* Lauren.

1b Are you from England?

b Watch video 1b and tick (✓) the correct answers.

1 Is Maibritt from England?
a ☐ Yes
b ☑ No
2 Is Euan from England?
a ☐ Yes
b ☐ No
3 Is Jenna from England?
a ☐ Yes
b ☐ No
4 Is Laura from England?
a ☐ Yes
b ☐ No
5 Is Ruby from England?
a ☐ Yes
b ☐ No

1c Are you a student?

c Watch video 1c. Match the people 1–5 with the sentences a–e.

1 [c] Maibritt
2 [ ] Euan
3 [ ] Jenna
4 [ ] Laura
5 [ ] Ruby

a I am. I study history at the University of York.
b No, I'm a manager.
c No, I'm not. I'm a teacher.
d No, I'm not a student, no. I am an editor.
e Yes, I am.

UNIT 2: All about me

2a Are you from a city, a town or a village?

a Watch video 2a and underline the correct words.

1 Sarah's from a *city* / *town* / *village*.
2 *It's* / *It isn't* near London.
3 Anna's from a *big town* / *small town* / *big city* / *small city*.
4 *It's* / *It isn't* near London.
5 Claire's from a *city* / *town* / *village*.
6 *It's* / *It isn't* near Cambridge.
7 Nino is from a *big town* / *small town* / *big city* / *small city*.
8 *It's* / *It isn't* in England.

2b What's in your bag?

b Watch video 2b. Match the people 1–4 with the objects a–d.

1 [d] Sarah
2 [ ] Anna
3 [ ] Claire
4 [ ] Nino

a an umbrella, a phone, some keys, an apple
b a bottle of water, a wallet, a phone, an umbrella
c a bottle of water, a photo, a newspaper
d a phone, some keys, a banana, a ticket

2c What's your surname?

c Watch video 2c and tick (✓) the correct answers.

1 Sarah ___________
a ☐ Greaves
b ☑ Grieves
c ☐ Greeves

2 Anna ___________
a ☐ Linter
b ☐ Linta
c ☐ Linthe

3 Claire ___________
a ☐ Barns
b ☐ Bahns
c ☐ Barnes

4 Nino ___________
a ☐ Chelidze
b ☐ Cheletse
c ☐ Shelitze

UNIT 3: Food and drink

3a Do you eat fruit every day?

a Watch video 3a and underline the correct words.

1 Euan: I *always* / *<u>usually</u>* / *sometimes* eat an apple or a banana at work.
2 Samantha: I *eat* / *don't eat* fruit every day.
3 Samantha: I *like* / *don't like* apples.
4 Colin: I *always* / *usually* / *sometimes* eat fruit once or twice a day.
5 Lauren: I usually have a banana for *breakfast* / *lunch*.

3b What time do you eat breakfast?

b Watch video 3b and tick (✓) the correct answers.

1 Euan: I usually eat breakfast at ___________.
a ☑ 7:00
b ☐ 7:30
c ☐ 8:00

2 Euan: I have dinner at ___________.
a ☐ 5:00 or 5:30
b ☐ 6:00 or 6:30
c ☐ 7:00 or 7:30

3 Samantha: I have lunch at ___________.
a ☐ 12:00
b ☐ 1:00
c ☐ 2:00

4 Samantha: I eat dinner at ___________.
a ☐ 5:30
b ☐ 6:30
c ☐ 7:30

5 Colin: I eat lunch at ___________.
a ☐ 12:00
b ☐ 1:00
c ☐ 2:00

6 Colin: I eat dinner at ___________.
a ☐ 5:00 or 5:30
b ☐ 6:30 or 7:00
c ☐ 5:00 or 7:00

7 Lauren: I have breakfast at ___________.
a ☐ 8:00
b ☐ 9:00
c ☐ 10:00

8 Lauren: I eat dinner at ___________.
a ☐ 5:00
b ☐ 6:00
c ☐ 7:00

3c Do you eat a big meal in the evening?

c Watch video 3c. Match the people 1–4 with the sentences a–d.

1 [b] Euan
2 ☐ Samantha
3 ☐ Colin
4 ☐ Lauren

a Yes. I usually eat fish and vegetables with rice or pasta.
b Yes. I like Indonesian, Chinese and Italian food.
c Yes. I eat spaghetti or meat and potatoes, or sometimes rice.
d Yes. I like lasagne.

UNIT 4: My life and my family

4a Where do you study?

a Watch video 4a. Match 1–4 with a–d to make sentences.

1 [b] Ruby
2 ☐ Lauren
3 ☐ Sarah
4 ☐ Jo

a studies at Bristol University. She studies Languages.
b studies at York University. She studies History.
c studies at Exeter University. She studies German.
d studies at Cambridge University.

4b Are you married?

b Watch video 4b and underline the correct words.

1 Ruby *is* / *<u>isn't</u>* married.
2 Lauren *is* / *isn't* married.
3 Sarah *is* / *isn't* married.
4 Sarah has *one child* / *two children*.
5 Jo *is* / *isn't* married.
6 Jo has *a son* / *a son and a daughter* / *four children*.

4c Do you have brothers and sisters?

c Watch video 4c and underline the correct words.

1 Ruby has four *brothers and one sister* / *sisters and one brother.*
2 They *are* / *aren't* married.
3 Lauren has one older *brother* / *sister.*
4 Lauren's brother *is* / *isn't* married.
5 Sarah has *two sisters and one brother* / *two brothers and one sister.*
6 They *are* / *aren't* married.
7 Jo has one *sister* / *brother.*
8 Jo's brother *is* / *isn't* married.
9 Jo's brother has *one girl and two boys* / *two girls and one boy.*

UNIT 5: Places

5a Is there a supermarket near here?

a Watch video 5a and underline the correct words.

1 Jo says there aren't any *supermarkets* / *cafés* / *hotels* near here.
2 Jason says there *is* / *isn't* a supermarket near here.
3 Jason says there isn't *a hotel* / *a café* near here.
4 Lauren says there's a supermarket and *a big café* / *a small café* near here.
5 Lauren says all the *hotels* / *good cafés* are in the centre of Cambridge.

5b Are there lots of houses in your street?

b Watch video 5b and tick (✓) the correct answers.

1 There are lots of houses in Jo's street.
a [✓] True
b [ ] False
2 There are new and old houses in Jo's street.
a [ ] True
b [ ] False
3 There are lots of houses in Jason's street.
a [ ] True
b [ ] False
4 There aren't any old houses in Jason's street.
a [ ] True
b [ ] False
5 There are lots of houses in Lauren's street.
a [ ] True
b [ ] False
6 There aren't any old houses in Lauren's street.
a [ ] True
b [ ] False

5c Are there any parks near your house?

c Watch video 5c. Match the people 1–4 with the sentences a–d.

1 [c] Jo
2 [ ] Jason
3 [ ] Maibritt
4 [ ] Lauren

a There isn't a park near the house.
b There's a big park in the next street. People play football and basketball there.
c There's a very large park near my house. I like going there.
d There's a big park. It has a playground and some sports fields.

UNIT 6: Work and routines

6a What do you do?

a Watch video 6a and underline the correct words.

1 Maibritt *works* / *doesn't work* in Cambridge.
2 Maibritt *works* / *doesn't work* long hours.
3 Matt *works* / *doesn't work* in Cambridge.
4 Matt *works* / *doesn't work* long hours.
5 Mark *has* / *doesn't have* a job in a restaurant.
6 Mark *works* / *doesn't work* long hours.
7 Laurence *works* / *doesn't work* in a factory.
8 Laurence *works* / *doesn't work* with computers.

6b When do you usually get up?

b Watch video 6b. Match the people 1–4 with the times a–d.

1 [b] Maibritt
2 [ ] Matt
3 [ ] Mark
4 [ ] Laurence

a 10:00 am
b 6:30 or 7:00 am
c 7:00 am
d 10:00 or 11:00 am

6c When do you usually go to work?

c Watch video 6c and tick (✓) the correct answers.

1 Maibritt goes to work at ________.
a [ ] 8:00 am
b [✓] 9:00 am
c [ ] 10:00 am
2 Matt goes to work at ________.
a [ ] 11:00 am
b [ ] 12:00 pm
c [ ] 1:00 pm
3 Mark goes to work at ________.
a [ ] 12:00 pm
b [ ] 1:00 pm
c [ ] 12:30 pm
4 Laurence goes to work at ________.
a [ ] 7:00 am
b [ ] 7:15 am
c [ ] 7:30 am

UNIT 7: Shopping and fashion

7a What's your favourite colour?

a Watch video 7a and tick (✓) the correct answers.

1 Anna's favourite colour is ____________.
a ☑ red
b ☐ green
c ☐ yellow

2 Anna often wears ____________.
a ☐ green, grey and brown
b ☐ purple and blue
c ☐ green, black and blue

3 Sarah's favourite colour is ____________.
a ☐ grey
b ☐ purple
c ☐ brown

4 Sarah often wears ____________.
a ☐ black and white
b ☐ black and blue
c ☐ black and purple

5 Claire's favourite colour is ____________.
a ☐ purple
b ☐ blue
c ☐ white

6 Claire often wears ____________.
a ☐ grey and purple
b ☐ green and purple
c ☐ grey and pale blue

7 Nino likes ____________.
a ☐ grey and blue
b ☐ white and yellow
c ☐ green and brown

8 Nino often wears ____________.
a ☐ brown and blue
b ☐ black and white
c ☐ red and black

9 Nino ____________ wears grey.
a ☐ always
b ☐ usually
c ☐ sometimes

7b Which clothes do you often wear together?

b Watch video 7b. Match 1–4 with a–d to make sentences.

1 [d] Anna often wears
2 ☐ Sarah often wears
3 ☐ Claire wears
4 ☐ Nino wears

a trousers, a top and a cardigan or a dress and a cardigan.
b a jumper, a skirt and a pair of boots.
c a skirt and blouse or a dress with high heels.
d jeans and a jumper or a T-shirt.

7c Do you like going shopping for clothes?

c Watch video 7c and underline the correct words.

1 Anna *likes / doesn't like* going shopping for clothes.
2 Sarah doesn't like going shopping for clothes because the shops are *expensive / busy / far away*.
3 Claire goes *to the town centre / online* to buy clothes.
4 Nino *likes / doesn't like* new clothes.

UNIT 8: Past events

8a Were you at home last weekend?

a Watch video 8a and tick (✓) the correct answers.

1 Ruby went to London on Saturday.
a ☑ True
b ☐ False

2 She was at home on Sunday.
a ☐ True
b ☐ False

3 Euan was at home on Sunday.
a ☐ True
b ☐ False

4 He went shopping on Sunday.
a ☐ True
b ☐ False

5 Maibritt wasn't at home at the weekend.
a ☐ True
b ☐ False

6 Laura was at home at the weekend.
a ☐ True
b ☐ False

8b Where were you at New Year?

b Watch video 8b and underline the correct words.

1 Ruby was *at home / at a party*.
2 Euan was *at home / at a party*.
3 Maibritt was *at home / at a party*.
4 Jenna was *at home / at a party*.
5 Laura was *at home / at a party*.

8c What free time activities were popular when you were a child?

c Watch video 8c. Match the people 1–5 with the free time activities a–e.

1 [e] Ruby
2 ☐ Euan
3 ☐ Maibritt
4 ☐ Jenna
5 ☐ Laura

a doing sport, playing outside in the street, playing with dolls and cars
b doing sport, reading, watching TV, playing music
c football, riding bikes, climbing trees
d playing outside, computer games, riding bikes, football
e reading, playing at the park with friends, computer games

UNIT 9: Holidays

9a Where did you go on holiday last year?

a Watch video 9a and tick (✓) the correct answers.

1 Euan went to Scotland ________.
a ☐ by plane
b ☑ by train

2 Euan ________ in a hotel.
a ☐ stayed
b ☐ didn't stay

3 It ________ sunny every day in Scotland.
a ☐ was
b ☐ wasn't

4 Samantha went to Turkey ________.
a ☐ by boat
b ☐ by plane

5 Samantha ________ in a hotel.
a ☐ stayed
b ☐ didn't stay

6 The weather in Turkey was ________ hot.
a ☐ quite
b ☐ very

7 Colin ________ to Portugal.
a ☐ flew
b ☐ took the train

8 Colin ________ in a hotel.
a ☐ stayed
b ☐ didn't stay

9 Lauren ________ in a big hotel in Rome.
a ☐ stayed
b ☐ didn't stay

10 It ________ hot and sunny every day in Rome.
a ☐ was
b ☐ wasn't

9b What did you do on holiday last year?

b Watch video 9b. Match 1–4 with a–d to make sentences.

1 [a] Euan
2 ☐ Samantha
3 ☐ Colin
4 ☐ Lauren

a visited family and stayed in a caravan.
b walked up mountains, swam in the sea and saw some amazing old buildings.
c saw a lot of old buildings and ate good food.
d went swimming and played tennis.

9c Did you enjoy your holiday last year?

c Watch video 9c and underline the correct words.

1 Euan *had* / *didn't have* a good time on holiday.
2 Euan's son *liked* / *didn't like* staying in a caravan.
3 Samantha *enjoyed* / *didn't enjoy* her holiday last year.
4 Samantha *liked* / *didn't like* the hot weather.
5 Colin *liked* / *didn't like* Portugal very much.
6 Lauren *enjoyed* / *didn't enjoy* her holiday last year.
7 Lauren *thought* / *didn't think* the holiday was very long.

UNIT 10: Here and now

10a Where do you eat your dinner?

a Watch video 10a and underline the correct words.

1 Ruby eats dinner in the *living room* / *dining room* / *kitchen*.
2 Sarah eats dinner in the *living room* / *dining room* / *kitchen*.
3 Jo eats dinner in the *living room* / *dining room* / *kitchen*.
4 Lauren eats dinner in the *living room* / *dining room* / *kitchen*.

10b Is there a TV in your home?

b Watch video 10b and tick (✓) the correct answers.

1 Ruby's family has a small TV.
a ☐ True
b ☑ False

2 Sarah has a TV in the dining room.
a ☐ True
b ☐ False

3 Jo has a TV in the living room.
a ☐ True
b ☐ False

4 Lauren has a new TV in the living room.
a ☐ True
b ☐ False

5 Lauren watches TV on the Internet.
a ☐ True
b ☐ False

10c Which room do you like best in your home?

c Watch video 10c. Match 1–4 with a–d to make sentences.

1 [b] Ruby likes
2 [ ] Sarah likes
3 [ ] Jo likes
4 [ ] Lauren likes

a her bedroom because all her things are there.
b the kitchen and she spends a lot of time there.
c the living room.
d the living room because it's quite big and there's lots of light.

UNIT 11: Achievers

11a Where did you grow up?

a Watch video 11a and underline the correct words.

1 Lauren *grew up* / *didn't grow up* in England.
2 Jason *grew up* / *didn't grow up* in England.
3 Maibritt *grew up* / *didn't grow up* in England.

11b Can you swim?

b Watch video 11b and underline the correct words.

1 Lauren *can swim very well* / *can swim quite well* / *can't swim at all.*
2 Jason *can swim* / *can't swim.*
3 Jo *can swim very well* / *can swim* / *can't swim at all.*
4 Maibritt likes swimming *at the beach* / *in swimming pools.*

11c Can you cook?

c Watch video 11c. Match 1–4 with a–d to make sentences.

1 [b] Lauren
2 [ ] Jason
3 [ ] Jo
4 [ ] Maibritt

a can make cakes, biscuits and bread.
b can cook but not very well.
c can cook traditional English food and curries.
d can cook lasagne.

UNIT 12: Plans

12a What are you going to do this evening?

a Watch video 12a and tick (✓) the correct answers.

1 Mark's going to go to ________.
a [ ] the beach
b [ ] the cinema
c [✓] the gym

2 Mark's going to have dinner ________.
a [ ] at home
b [ ] at a friend's house
c [ ] at a restaurant

3 Maibritt's going to ________ and then watch TV.
a [ ] cook dinner
b [ ] do yoga
c [ ] clean her house

4 Laurence is going to ________ some friends.
a [ ] go to a restaurant with
b [ ] cook dinner for
c [ ] do sport with

5 Matt's going to ________ his sister.
a [ ] have a party for
b [ ] meet
c [ ] phone

12b What are you going to do tomorrow?

b Watch video 12b. Match the people 1–4 with their plans a–d.

1 [c] Mark
2 [ ] Maibritt
3 [ ] Laurence
4 [ ] Matt

a I'm going to celebrate my son's birthday.
b I'm going to go for a run.
c I'm going to work.
d I'm going to work.

12c Where are you going to go on your next holiday?

c Watch video 12c and underline the correct words.

1 Mark *is* / *isn't* going to stay in a hotel in Italy.
2 Mark's going to go to the beach and *do a lot of sport* / *go swimming* / *relax.*
3 Maibritt *is* / *isn't* going to stay in a hotel in Denmark.
4 Maibritt's going to visit *her mum* / *lots of museums* / *some friends.*
5 Laurence *is* / *isn't* going to stay in a hotel in France.
6 Laurence is going to *visit some friends* / *go walking* / *do yoga* and have barbecues.
7 Matt's going to stay *in a small hotel* / *on a campsite* / *with his cousin* by the beach.
8 Matt's going to *have barbecues* / *eat at nice restaurants* / *make nice meals.*

AUDIOSCRIPTS

Unit 1

01.01

A Hi. I'm Hakan. What are your names?

B Hi. I'm Carmen.

C And I'm Camila.

A Nice to meet you. Are you from the USA?

B No, we're from Spain. We're Spanish.

01.02

1 **A** This is my friend Maribel.

B Where's she from? Is she Brazilian?

A No, she isn't. She's from Spain.

2 **C** Who are Serena and Venus? Are they volleyball players?

D No, they aren't. They're tennis players.

C Are they British?

D No, they aren't. They're American.

01.03

1 British	6 Turkish
2 Australian	7 Japanese
3 Chinese	8 Spanish
4 Italian	9 American
5 Brazilian	10 Mexican

01.04

1 **DEBBIE** Good morning! How are you today?

AYLA I'm not bad, thanks. And you?

D I'm OK, thanks.

2 **JENNY** Good afternoon, Dean.

DEAN Hi Jenny. This is my friend Becky.

J Hi Becky. How are you?

BECKY I'm good, thank you. Nice to meet you.

01.05

CARLA Good afternoon. My name's Carla Watkins.

JAMES Hello. I'm James Hargreaves.

C Nice to meet you, James.

J Nice to meet you, too.

C Oh, Greg! This is James Hargreaves from Electric Blue Technology.

GREG Hello James! How are you?

J I'm fine, thank you. And you?

G I'm good, thanks.

01.06

1 **A** How are you?

2 **B** I'm fine, thanks.

3 **A** So, this is your office.

4 **B** Good evening!

5 **A** I'm Andy and this is Gaston.

6 **B** Nice to meet you.

01.07

RYAN Good morning. Is this the teachers' room?

ALICE Yes, it is. Are you a new student?

R No, I'm not. I'm a new teacher.

A Oh, are you Ryan?

R Yes, Ryan Robson.

A It's nice to meet you, Ryan. I'm Alice Long, the school manager.

R Nice to meet you, too.

A Where are you from, Ryan?

R I'm from Leeds, in England, in the UK.

A Oh, right.

R And you?

A I'm from Boston, in the USA.

R Really? Boston's a nice city.

A Well, your class is 1A.

R OK.

A This is the class list. It's a small class. There are eight students.

R What countries are they from?

A Let's see. Errrr.... Ana and Sofia are from Italy. Lee and Ping are from China. Daniela is from Brazil and Manuel is Spanish.

R And Alim and Fehim. Those are Turkish names. Are they from Turkey?

A Yes, that's right. OK, this is your desk and here are your books ...

Unit 2

02.01

1 where	3 what	5 his	7 hello
2 he	4 who	6 her	8 when

02.02

1 I have eighty books.

2 Thirty apples, please.

3 I have six bags.

4 Twelve eggs, please.

5 Do you have fifty tickets?

6 Fourteen bottles of water, please.

02.03

1 knives	4 newspapers	7 watches
2 villages	5 tickets	8 bottles
3 students	6 books	9 houses

02.04

A What's your surname?

B It's Milner.

A How do you spell that?

B M-I-L-N-E-R.

A What's your address?

B It's 39 Oak Street, Brighton.

A What's your phone number?

B It's 07896 7421019.

02.05

A What's your surname?

B It's Gibbins.

A How do you spell that?

B G-I-B-B-I-N-S.

A What's your phone number?

B It's 09745 833081.

A What's your email address?

B It's alice-eight-eight-eight at zipmail dot com.

02.06

1 How are you?

2 Is it a village?

3 What's your surname?

4 What's your address?

5 Can you spell that?

6 What's the spelling?

7 Are you from a big city?

8 Is this your phone?

9 Where are you from?

10 What's your email address?

02.07

DARREN I'm Darren. I'm the manager of a TV shop in Manchester. I don't have an office, but I have a chair and a desk in the shop. It's an old desk and it isn't big, but I have a phone, a computer and a newspaper on my desk, and the keys to the shop.

PAULA I'm Paula. I'm a teacher in Washington. I have three desks: one at home, one in the teachers' room at the school and one in my classroom. I have a laptop and some books on my desk in the teachers' room, but I don't have a phone. Today, my bag is on my desk with my umbrella.

JAMIE I'm Jamie. I'm a student in Southampton. I have a desk at school and another desk in my bedroom where I do my homework. I have a computer on my desk at home, and today I also have an apple and a knife, and a glass of water.

Unit 3

03.01

1 We eat fruit every day.

2 Do you eat bread?

3 They don't eat eggs.

4 **A** Do you like vegetables?

B No, I don't.

5 Do you like fish?

6 **A** Do you like meat?

B No, we don't.

7 I don't like rice.

8 **A** Do you like fruit?

B Yes, I do.

03.02

DUNCAN Mmm! I like meat! I eat meat every day!

RAJIT Really? I don't eat meat.

D Oh, you don't eat meat. Do you eat fish?

R No, I don't.

D Do you eat eggs?

R Yes, I do. I like eggs.

03.03

1 my	4 rice	7 I	10 Italy
2 tea	5 milk	8 we	11 meat
3 this	6 is	9 like	12 key

03.04

1 **A** What fruit do you like?

B Apples and bananas.

2 **A** Would you like a biscuit with your coffee?

B No, thanks.

3 **A** A tomato is a vegetable.

B No, it isn't. It's a fruit!

4 **A** We have bread, butter and eggs.

B Good! An egg sandwich for me, please.

5 **A** A cheese and tomato pizza, please.

B Certainly.

6 **A** Is this fruit juice?

B Yes, it's orange juice.

03.05

1 eight o'clock	5 half past ten
2 quarter past seven	6 quarter to one
3 eleven o'clock	7 quarter to six
4 quarter past one	8 half past one

03.06

1 morning	6 four
2 afternoon	7 water
3 half	8 class
4 past	9 banana
5 always	10 small

03.07

WAITRESS Good morning.

NANCY Hello. I'd like a piece of fruit cake, please.

W Certainly. And to drink?

N Can I have a cup of coffee, please?

W Of course. With milk?

N No, thanks.

W Here you are. That's £6.50, please.

N OK. Thank you very much.

W Thank you.

03.08

WAITER Good afternoon.

SAM Hello. I'd like a cup of tea, please.

W Sure. And to eat?

S I'd like a cheese sandwich, please.

W With tomato?

S No, thanks. And can I have some chocolate cake and a glass of water too, please?

W Of course! That's £11, please.

S OK. Here you are.

W Thank you.

03.09

1 a slice of pizza

2 a cup of coffee

3 a glass of water

4 a piece of cheese

5 a glass of fruit juice

6 a cup of tea

7 a glass of milk

8 a piece of chocolate cake

03.10

ANNA What do you want, John?
JOHN A sandwich. What sandwiches do they have?
A They have cheese.
J Oh, I never eat cheese. I don't like it.
A Really? Do you like eggs?
J Oh, yes. I like eggs.
A And tomatoes?
J Yes, I eat a lot of tomatoes.
A OK. They have egg and tomato sandwiches. I like those.
J Great. So, two egg and tomato sandwiches.
A Do they have any cake?
J Yes, they have chocolate cake or apple pie with ice cream.
A Well, I don't eat a lot of chocolate, but I like chocolate cake.
J Me, too. And to drink? Tea or coffee? I usually drink tea.
A I don't like hot drinks. Do they have fruit juice?
J Yes, apple juice or orange juice.
A Oh, apple juice. I always have orange juice for breakfast.
J OK. Excuse me ...

Unit 4

04.01

1 Where do you live?
2 Do you speak French?
3 Do you work in a factory?
4 What do you study?
5 Do you go to the gym?
6 When do you have lunch?

04.02

1 she	4 father	7 they	9 eight
2 that	5 mother	8 the	10 brother
3 right	6 three		

04.03

CATH Do you have photos of your home?
AMY Yes, I do.
C Can I see them?
A Sure. This is my flat.
C Who's this?
A My brother Harry.
C Great photo!
A Thanks. Here's another picture of my flat.
C It's really nice.

04.04

JENNY Do you have photos of your family?
SEAN Yes, I do.
J Can I see them?
S Sure. This is my dad and my brother.
J Nice picture!
S And this is me with my mum and my sister.
J They're lovely! Thank you.

04.05

1 orange	5 child	9 picture
2 question	6 Japan	10 watch
3 cheap	7 vegetable	
4 page	8 manager	

04.06

BOB Hi, Kerry!
KERRY Hello, Bob. It's so nice to see you! How are you?
B I'm fine, thanks. I'm a student at London University now.
K Really? What subject do you study?
B Business.
K Do you like it?
B I love it.
K And where do you live?
B In a house with two other students. And you?
K I live in Hong Kong now and I work in an office at the university.
B Really? Do you speak Chinese?
K Well, I have Chinese classes. My Chinese isn't very good, but I speak English at work.
B So why are you in England now?
K I'm on holiday. I'm here to see my family.
B How are your mum and dad?
K They're well, thanks. How are your parents?
B They're fine. They live in France now, near Paris.
K Wow, that's great. Hey, look, is that Ali over there? Ali! ... Ali! ...

Unit 5

05.01

1 There's one school here.
2 There are two teachers.
3 There are a few cars.
4 There's a small museum.
5 There are ten families.
6 There's an old hospital.

05.02

1 few	5 school	9 love
2 butter	6 study	10 who
3 sometimes	7 beautiful	11 funny
4 supermarket	8 food	12 mother

05.03

1 **A** Is there a bath in the room?
B No, there isn't. But there is a shower.
2 **A** There aren't any hotels in this town.
B Oh!
A There's a hostel on King Street. It's very good.
B OK. Thanks.
3 **B** Is there a car park for this hotel?
A Yes, there is.
B Are there any empty rooms on the ground floor?
A No, there aren't. Sorry. There are a lot of empty rooms on the top floor.
B Oh ... No thanks.

05.04

1 bath	5 she	9 museum
2 shower	6 sure	10 shop
3 China	7 six	11 station
4 Turkish	8 finish	12 cinema

05.05

A Excuse me, can you help me?
B Yes, of course.
A Is there a cinema near here?
B No, I'm sorry. There aren't any cinemas near here. But there are two in the city centre.
A OK. And is there a museum near here?
B Yes, there is. It's in this street. Just over there.
A Oh yes! Great! Thanks for your help.
B No problem.

05.06

A Excuse me, can you help me?
B Yes, of course.
A Are there any hotels near here?
B Yes, there are. There's one in the next street.
A Oh, good. And are there any hostels – cheap hostels?
B No, I'm sorry. There aren't.
A OK. Thanks for your help.
B No problem.

05.07

1 It's a very good hotel.
2 It's so hot today!
3 I'm really sorry.
4 This room's really nice.
5 It's a very big school.
6 This TV is so old!
7 The museum's really boring.
8 The car park's very small.

05.08

RECEPTIONIST Good morning. Can I help?
HARRY Hi. I'd like a hotel room for the weekend.
R Well, there are a lot of different hotels and they have different prices.
H I'd like a room for one person near the beach.
R Hmm, it's summer and there aren't a lot of free rooms. The Hotel Casa is near the beach. They have rooms with baths for $160 a day and breakfast is free. The rooms have TVs and free wi-fi, and there's a good restaurant in the hotel.
H It's very expensive and I don't have a lot of money.
R Well, there's the City Hostel near the station. The rooms are small, but they're clean and a room for one person is only $40.
H That's cheap.
R Yes, it is. There are showers in all the rooms and wi-fi in the café on the ground floor, but you have to pay for the wi-fi. A lot of backpackers stay there and it's very friendly.
H Is there a restaurant?
R No, there isn't. But there's a café and there are two supermarkets near the hostel.
H OK.
R Do you want me to phone the hostel?
H Yes, please.

Unit 6

06.01

1 Hello, I'm Natasha. I'm the hotel receptionist.
2 **A** What's your brother's job?
B He's a businessman.
3 I'm an IT worker. I work with computers.
4 I'm a taxi driver. I sometimes work at night.
5 I work in this restaurant. I'm a chef.
6 Lionel Messi is a football player.
7 **A** What's your sister's job?
B She's a waitress.
8 **A** Excuse me! Are you a shop assistant?
B Yes, I am. Can I help you?

06.02

1 park	5 sport	9 fruit
2 here	6 work	10 Turkey
3 girl	7 thirty	11 wrong
4 world	8 thirteen	12 university

06.03

1 **A** Where does Lottie live?
B In Australia.
2 **A** Does your husband work at night?
B No, he doesn't.
3 When does Martin get home?
4 What time does she wake up in the morning?
5 When do Rosa and Luca finish work?
6 **A** Does he study Spanish?
B Yes, he does.

06.04

1 I wake up at 7:00 am and I get up at 7:15 am.
2 I have breakfast at home.
3 I go to work every day.
4 I start work at 9:00 am and I finish work at 5:30 pm.
5 I arrive home at 6:30 pm.
6 I go to bed at 11:00 pm.

06.05

1 twenty	3 Spanish	5 fruit
2 breakfast	4 play	6 class

06.06

DAN Would you like a cup of tea?
EVA Yes, please.
D And would you like a piece of cake?
E No, it's OK, thanks.
D I need to go to the shops for bread.
E I'll come with you.
D That's great, thanks. And I need to make some sandwiches.
E I'll help you.
D Thank you, that's very kind.

06.07

MEG Would you like a cup of coffee, Rob?
ROB Yes, please.
M And would you like a piece of cake?
R No, I'm fine, thanks – just coffee, please.
M I need to make lunch for Jake and Carrie.
R I'll help you.
M All right. Thanks. We need pizzas.
R I can make pizzas. I make very good pizzas!
M Don't worry. It's OK. The pizzas at the supermarket are fine.
R OK, I'll go to the supermarket.
M Thank you. That's great.

06.08

1 **A** I need to make dinner for eight people!
B I can help you.
2 **A** I need to go to the supermarket, but I'm really busy.
B I'll go.
3 **A** Oh no! I don't have any money with me!
B I can pay.
4 **A** I can't open this bottle of water!
B I'll do it.

5 **A** I need to go to the shops. Can you drive me?
B Sorry, but I'm really busy. Jim can take you.
6 **A** I need some cups. Do you have any cups?
B No, I don't. I can give you some glasses.

06.09

PRESENTER Welcome to the show. This week we're talking to people who live and work in Scotland. Today, my guest is 44-year-old Ian Baker. Which part of Scotland are you from, Ian?
IAN I'm from a village near Aberdeen.
P And what do you do?
I Well, I'm a businessman. My wife Rita and I have a factory in Aberdeen.
P That's interesting. How many people work there?
I We have 90 workers.
P And what do you make?
I Computers for schools.
P Do you like your work?
I Yes, I do. I work long hours. I start at 7 or 8 in the morning and finish at 7 or 8 in the evening. But my job is never boring. I'm not in my office every day. I go to different places and I meet a lot of people, like the teachers and children who use our computers.
P Are all your customers here in the UK?
I No, some customers are here, but schools in South America also buy our computers, so I often fly to Brazil for meetings.
P Are your meetings in English?
I Sometimes, but we usually speak in Portuguese.
P Does your wife go with you?
I No, she works with our customers in the UK and the rest of Europe.
P And how often do you ...

Unit 7

07.01

1 Do you like these flowers?
2 Do you like those flowers?
3 I'd like that car.
4 I want this car!

07.02

1 This glass is ten euros fifty.
2 This foot ball is thirty pounds.
3 That guitar is one hundred and twenty-nine dollars ninety-nine.
4 That picture is twenty-four euros seventy-five.
5 Those cups are nine pounds fifty.
6 These plants are three dollars eighty-nine.

07.03

1 ball	5 plate	9 cup
2 suitcase	6 lamp	10 plant
3 glass	7 guitar	
4 bag	8 book	

07.04

1 It's Kate's bag.
2 They're Peter's jeans.
3 My friend's jacket is brown.
4 The boys' trousers are new.
5 I never wear a hat.
6 I sometimes wear my sister's clothes.

07.05

1 jeans	5 international	9 Germany
2 large	6 Japanese	10 sugar
3 fashion	7 vegetables	11 village
4 shoes	8 shirt	12 shop

07.06

1 **A** That's £52.95, please.
B Can I use a card to pay?
A Yes. Enter your PIN, please.
2 **A** Can I help you?
B Can I look around?
A Of course.
3 **A** Here's your receipt.
B Thanks.
4 **A** How much are these bags?
B They're £35 each.
5 **A** I'd like that T-shirt, please.
B Certainly. Here you are.

07.07

SHOP ASSISTANT Can I help you?
CUSTOMER Yes, how much are these white plates?
SA They're £4 each.
C OK, I'd like four white plates, please.
SA Certainly. That's £16, please.
C Can I use a card to pay?
SA Of course. Enter your PIN, please. OK, here's your receipt. Would you like a bag?
C No, don't worry.
SA OK, here you are.
C Thank you very much.
SA Thank you.

07.08

1 Here you are.
2 Is it blue or green?
3 Three apples, please.
4 Are you OK?
5 She only wears white.
6 These cups are for me and you.
7 He always wears black.
8 There are two empty bags.

07.09

PAUL Why do we have to go shopping, Sue? It's so boring.
SUE You know why, Paul. It's your mum's birthday on Sunday. We need to find a present for her.
P That's easy. I always buy a box of chocolates and some flowers from that shop near the station.
S Chocolates and flowers? Those are boring. Let's get something useful for her new flat.
P Oh, right. Well, let's try this store here. They sell lots of nice things.
S OK. Look, these cups and plates are nice. They have pictures of cats on them.
P Mum has a lot of cups. I don't think she needs any more.
S Well, what about a clock? Those clocks over there are nice ... Or how about a new lamp? This one is good for reading and your mum loves reading.
P A lamp is a good idea. I don't like the colour, though. Do they have any other colours?
S I don't think so. They're all brown.
P Oh, right ... Hey, do you like those little red tables over there? I know Mum wants a new table for her laptop.
S Oh, that's a good idea. How much are they?
P £60 each.
S OK, let's get one. And next, we need to go to the card shop and choose a birthday card ...

Unit 8

08.01

A You weren't here on Friday afternoon. Where were you?
B I was with my brothers. We were at a basketball game.
A Oh, was it good?
B No, it wasn't. I don't like basketball.
A Oh. And where were you on Friday evening?
B We were at a party.
A Was it a good party?
B It was OK. The people were really nice, but the music wasn't very good.

08.02

1 It's January 2021. It was January 2020 a year ago.
2 Today it's Monday, the fourth of January. Yesterday, it was the third of January.
3 It's Monday evening. I was at work from two pm until five thirty pm. I was at work this afternoon.
4 It's Monday evening. I was at work from eight thirty am until eleven thirty am. I was at work this morning.
5 It's Monday. I was at work from eight pm until eleven thirty pm on Sunday. I was at work last night.
6 It's January 2021. I was in Brazil in December 2020. I was in Brazil last month.

08.03

1 James was at home.
2 We were in Brighton
3 You were at work.
4 My parents were in Australia.
5 The party was fun.
6 The match was exciting.
7 The concert was good.
8 The meetings were interesting.

08.04

1 I read the news online every day.
2 I sometimes watch films on my phone.
3 I never go to the cinema.
4 I don't read magazines.
5 I have a shower every evening.
6 I usually listen to a podcast in the morning.
7 I often watch football matches on TV.
8 I play video games every day.
9 I always listen to music in the evening.
10 I always go to parties at the weekend.

08.05

1 talked	5 played
2 called	6 watched
3 tried	7 looked
4 listened	8 lived

08.06

ANGELA I went to the beach last week. It was great.
SOL Oh, let's go to the beach together some time!
A That's a lovely idea.
S We could go this weekend.
A I'm sorry, I'm busy with my family this weekend.
S OK. Shall we go next Saturday?
A I can't go on Saturday, but I'm free on Sunday. I can go on Sunday.
S OK, Sunday. Good.
A Great!

08.07

DAVID Shall we go for a coffee?
KYOKO Coffee? Good idea!
D Great! Let's go now.
K I'm sorry, I can't go now. I have a meeting at ten o'clock.
D OK. We could go at eleven o'clock.
K Great! Shall we go to the new Italian café?
D OK, that's a nice idea! See you at eleven.

08.08

1 Shall we go for a meal tomorrow?
2 That's a lovely idea.
3 Let's go to the cinema next week.
4 That's a great idea.
5 I'm away on Tuesday.
6 That's a nice idea.

08.09

GRACE Morning, Matt. How was your weekend?
MATT It was good, thanks, Grace. My wife was at work on Saturday, so I was at home with the children. I think they were a bit bored. But we went to a concert in the park yesterday. There were a lot of people.
G Really? How was the concert?
M It was fun. The bands were very good.
G Was it expensive?
M Well, that was the best thing. A family ticket was only £10.00! We had a great day. There was a lot to see and do. Anyway, how was your weekend?
G Oh, it was good. I was in Barcelona.
M Wow! Was it your first visit to Barcelona?
G No, my sister moved there four years ago and I often visit her.
M Was it hot?
G It wasn't hot, but it wasn't very cold either. On Saturday, we went to a restaurant on the beach. We had a lovely meal there, but the restaurant was empty! There weren't any other people.
M What did you do yesterday?
G We went to the National Museum. It was really interesting. We saw so many things.
M How much was it?
G It was free. You don't have to pay to go into some museums on Sunday.

Unit 9

09.01

1 **A** Our father went to Los Angeles last week. He stayed at a hotel, I think.
B No, he didn't stay at a hotel. He stayed at a campsite.
2 **A** We visited a lot of museums on holiday.
B We didn't visit a lot of museums. We visited two museums! That's not a lot!
3 **A** How was the café?
B I went to the office! I didn't go to a café!
4 **A** They had a car on holiday in France.
B Well, no, they didn't have a car. They had bikes.
5 **A** I bought a few new clothes yesterday.
B You didn't buy a few new clothes! You bought a lot of new clothes!
6 **A** I read a lot of books last weekend.
B You didn't read a lot of books. You read one book! That's all!

09.02

1 what	5 train	9 watch
2 taxi	6 father	10 want
3 car	7 take	11 camp
4 flat	8 plane	12 garden

09.03

A What did you do on New Year's Eve? Did you go out?
B No, I didn't. I stayed at home.
A Really? Why did you stay at home?
B I wasn't very well.
A Oh, no! Did Jack stay at home?
B No, he didn't. He went into the city.
A Did he see the fireworks?
B Yes, he did.
A What time did he get home?
B I don't know. I was in bed!

09.04

1 **A** It's –7°C! I don't like winter!
B Really? I like this season. I like cold weather and I really like snow!
2 **A** It's really windy today.
B Yes, there's always a lot of wind in the autumn.
3 **A** Look at the rain!
B I know. It often rains in this country.
4 **A** Did you have good weather on holiday? It was 42°C here.
B 42°C! It wasn't hot, but it was warm and sunny every day.

09.05

1 cloud	5 town	9 doctor
2 hot	6 cold	10 brown
3 snowy	7 phone	11 wrong
4 holiday	8 ago	12 trousers

09.06

1 **A** Can you go to the shops? We need bread.
B Sorry, I'm really busy.
A Oh, OK, I'll do it then.
2 **A** Can you do something for me?
B Sure, what is it?
A Could you meet me at the station on Sunday?
B Yes, certainly.
A Thanks, that's really kind of you.
3 **A** Can you come to the shops with me today?
B Sorry, I can't. I'm really busy.
A Oh, OK. Could you come with me tomorrow?
B Sure, no problem.
A Thanks.

09.07

KARINA Hi Saúl.
SAÚL Hi Karina. How are you?
K I'm fine, thanks. Could you do something for me?
S Yes, of course. What is it?
K Can you pick Jenny up from school at four?
S Sure, no problem.
K Thanks, that's really kind of you.
S That's OK. See you later.
K See you later.

09.08

1 lovely	5 autumn	9 restaurant
2 expensive	6 different	10 interesting
3 beautiful	7 museum	11 holiday
4 station	8 cinema	12 campsite

09.09

RESEARCHER Excuse me, sir. Do you have time to answer a holiday questionnaire?
MAN IN STREET Er, yes. OK.
R Thank you. Right, my first question is: When was your last holiday?
M Oh, in autumn. We usually go on holiday in summer, but this year we went in autumn.
R Did you stay in the UK or did you go to another country?
M I went to Faro in Portugal with my wife. The children didn't want to come, so they stayed at home.
R How did you get there?
M Well my wife doesn't like flying, so we went by ship from England to Spain, then we took a train to Faro.
R How long was your holiday?
M Three weeks.
R Did you stay in a hotel?
M No, we didn't. One of our friends has a house near the beach and we stayed there. It was our second holiday there.
R Do you speak Portuguese?
M No, but I learned a few phrases before we left England.
R Why didn't you stay in the UK for your holiday?
M Because Portugal has better weather! England is often cold and rainy in autumn.
R OK, and my next question …

Unit 10

10.01

1 bathroom	5 ninth
2 kitchen	6 month
3 picture	7 question
4 chair	8 thirty

10.02

1 Who are you phoning?
2 We aren't studying.
3 Why is Emir talking on the phone?
4 I'm not reading this book.
5 Are your friends waiting for the bus?
6 Greta isn't staying at the hotel.

10.03

ANDY Hi, it's me. Where are you? What are you doing?
TILDA I'm with Jenny and Craig.
A Oh, are you working?
T Yes, we are. Can I have some apple juice, please?
A Apple juice? What are you talking about?
T Sorry, I'm not talking to you. I'm talking to the waiter, but he isn't listening.
A Waiter? Is there a waiter at work?
T No, we aren't working in the office. We're in a meeting at a café.
A Oh …

10.04

1 **A** Where are you? Are you at the airport?
B No, I'm in a restaurant with Marco!
2 **A** Is Pasha at work?
B No, he's on holiday.
3 **A** You could phone Isabella. She's at home.
B I don't have my phone. It's in the car.
4 **A** Is Emma at school?
B No, she's in bed.
5 **A** Are you on the bus?
B No, there aren't any buses. I'm in a taxi.
6 **A** I'm still at the station. The train's late.
B Oh dear. Can you text me when you're on the train?

10.05

1 husband	6 ago
2 picture	7 Japanese
3 Brazil	8 hospital
4 daughter	9 computer
5 autumn	10 afternoon

10.06

A Oh, excuse me!
B Yes? How can I help?
A What time's the next bus to Seville?
B It's at 11:15.
A So it leaves in ten minutes. Is it a direct bus?
B No, you change at Córdoba.
A OK, and which bus stop is it?
B Number two, near the ticket office.
A Great! Thanks for your help.
B No problem.

10.07

A Excuse me.
B Yes? How can I help?
A What time's the next train to Eastbourne?
B The next train leaves in half an hour.
A So at 10:25. Is it a direct train?
B No, you change at Brighton.
A OK, and which platform is it?
B It's platform nine.
A Great! Thanks for your help.
B No problem.

10.08

1 pair	4 meal	7 here	9 where
2 wear	5 there	8 chair	10 clear
3 we're	6 year		

10.09

JACK Hi, Mum.
MUM Hello, Jack. Is Dad home yet?
J No, there's no one here except me. Dad phoned from his office half an hour ago. There's a problem so he's working late.
M What are you doing? I can hear music. Are you watching TV?
J No, I'm listening to music and getting ready to go out to the cinema.
M And where's Melinda?
J She's at the sports centre with some of her friends. I think they're playing tennis. What about you?
M I'm at the station with your brother. We're waiting for the train, but there's a problem.
J What do you mean?
M Well, the train is late and it's starting to snow now.
J Oh, no!
M Tim isn't very happy. He's only wearing his jeans and a jumper. He didn't want to put his coat on when we left the house.
J Can I talk to him?
M Not now. He's in the café. He's buying some hot drinks for us.
J Oh, right.
M Oh, I've got to go! The train is arriving. There are lots of people here on the platform and it's going to be difficult to get a seat. Tim! Tim! Hurry up!

Unit 11

11.01

A I've got some photos of the party. They're very funny.
B Oh, can I see them?
A Yes, just a minute … OK … My brother's in this picture. He arrived really late.
B Really? Where is he? I can't see him!
A He's there, with the blue hat!
B Oh yes! It's a very big hat! Is that you? It's your T-shirt.
A Yes, that's me. I'm with Ian and Debbie. They're really nice.
B And who's that?
A That's Anna-Maria. She's at our house now. She's staying with us.
B Can I meet her?
A Yes, of course. She really wants to meet you!

11.02

1 work	sport	shirt
2 daughter	thirty	Thursday
3 university	early	near
4 born	first	world
5 people	person	girl
6 Turkish	grow	weren't

11.03

1 Your pictures are beautiful! You can paint very well.
2 **A** Can you cook?
B Yes, I can.
3 I like music, but I can't sing at all! I'm a terrible singer!
4 Jenny can speak Spanish very well.
5 **A** Can he run 10 km?
B No, he can't.
6 They're good swimmers. They can swim very well.

11.04

1 Can you ride a horse?
2 When did you last paint a picture?
3 How often do you cook a meal for a lot of people?
4 You're at a party and you like the music. Do you dance?
5 Did you sing a song yesterday?
6 Can you run 5 km?
7 Do people swim in the sea in your country?
8 How often do you drive a car?

11.05

1 I can swim.
2 Can you drive?
3 Yes, I can.
4 Jim can't sing.
5 Can he dance?
6 No, he can't.

11.06

1 **A** What do you think of this room?
B I don't think grey is a good idea for the walls.
A Maybe you're right. But I think it's OK with the red bed.
B I'm not so sure.
2 **A** What did you think of the film?
B It was terrible!
C Yes, I agree. It's a really bad film!
A Really? I don't think so. I liked it.

11.07

MATEO What do you think of my new car?
CARMEN I think it's really nice.
PHILIP I'm not so sure.
C Why not?
P I don't think yellow is a very good colour.
M Maybe you're right.
P Mm.
M What did you think of my old car?

11.08

1	tourist	stay	5	think	bank
2	engineer	enjoy	6	listened	find
3	answer	dance	7	clocks	six
4	school	ask	8	interesting	paint

11.09

ALEX What are you doing, Camila?
CAMILA Hi Alex. I'm working.
A You're looking at job websites! I hope your manager doesn't see you.
C He isn't in the office.
A Good! Let me see the website. Look! There's a job for a singer on a ship … but you can't sing. Oh, and there's a job for a chef on the same ship. You're a fantastic cook.
C Just one small problem. I can't swim so I don't want to work on a boat.
A Well, what about this job as an English teacher in Mexico? You speak Spanish and you love travelling.
C But I can't teach and I don't want to live in a really hot country.
A Oh, right. Well, an IT company in Manchester wants a receptionist.
C I don't want to work in another office.
A How about this job as a tour guide? You take people on bus tours around York.
C Hmm ... Sounds interesting. What do they want?
A Someone who knows a lot about York and who can speak English and another language.
C Well I was born in York, so I know a lot about it, but I can't drive.
A You don't drive the bus. You just talk to the passengers.
C Oh, right. Well, that sounds interesting. I'll phone the tour company this afternoon!
A Shhh! Your manager's coming back.

Unit 12

12.01

1 **A** Is there an email from Stephen? He's going to write to you with information about the boat trip.
B I don't know. I'm not going to check my emails today or tomorrow.
A Oh, OK. Well, I'm going to phone him this evening, so I can ask him then.
2 **A** It's the holidays! I'm going to sleep for ten hours every night! I'm going to watch TV every day!
B Really? That's so boring! My brother and I are going to work on a farm near the mountains. The people there are going to teach us how to ride horses.
A Hmm, sounds quite interesting. What about your sister?
B She isn't going to come with us. She wants to stay at home.

12.02

first	fifth	sixteenth
second	ninth	twentieth
third	twelfth	twenty-second
fourth	thirteenth	thirty-first

12.03

1 You're going to stay at a hotel.
2 They're going to live in Canada.
3 Anna's going to do her homework.
4 I'm going to check my emails.
5 He's going to listen to music.
6 I'm going to read a book.

12.04

1 When are we going to meet for coffee?
2 Is he going to have lunch at home?
3 Where are they going to get married?
4 Are you going to drive to the station tomorrow?
5 What's she going to do this evening?
6 How are you going to cook the potatoes?

12.05

1 **A** What are you going to do this morning?
B I'm going to clean the house – and you're going to help me!
2 **A** So, is he going to play the piano this evening?
B Yes, he is. Are you going to listen?
3 **A** What are you and your friends going to do in the holidays?
B I don't know. We're going to talk about it this afternoon.
4 **A** Where's she going to watch TV?
B In the living room.
5 When am I going to do all these things on my list?

12.06

1	wall	5	November	9	windy
2	evening	6	volleyball	10	winter
3	wi-fi	7	warm	11	weekend
4	visit	8	drive	12	invite

12.07

A Would you like to go to a concert this evening?
B I'd love to, but I have lots of homework for tomorrow.
A You're a good student! Are you free tomorrow night?
B Yes, I am.
A Would you like to go to the cinema?
B Yes, I'd love to. Thank you.

12.08

A Would you like to come for dinner tomorrow night?
B Sorry, I'm busy then.
A Are you free on Friday?
B No, sorry. I'm busy on Friday, too. But Saturday's OK.
A Great! You can come on Saturday.
B Thank you!

12.09

1 **A** Would you like to come to my party on Saturday?
B I'd love to come. Thank you.
2 **A** Would you like to go to the cinema on Thursday?
B Sorry, I'm busy then. But Friday's OK.
A OK, we can go on Friday.
B Great!
3 **A** Would you like to come for lunch at the weekend?
B I'd love to, but I'm away this weekend.
A Are you free next weekend?
B Yes, I am.
A You can come then!
B Thank you. I'd love to come.

12.10

1	book	4	school	7	cook
2	pool	5	food	8	look
3	good	6	boots	9	afternoon

12.11

MARTA Hi, Lucas. Can you hear me?
LUCAS Hi, Marta. Yes, I can see you and hear you. Where are you now?
M I'm in Los Angeles for three days. I took the bus from San Diego yesterday.
L What are you going to do there?
M Well, today after breakfast, I'm going to visit a film studio and go shopping in Rodeo Drive.
L Wow! Rodeo Drive is expensive.
M I just want to look around. Maybe I'll see someone famous! What about you?
L It's not raining here, so I'm going to take the dog for a walk. Then I'm going to have dinner and read a book.
M What about Mum and Dad? Are they at home with you?
L Mum's here, but she's in the shower. She's going to meet some friends later and go to the cinema. Dad went out a few minutes ago. He's going to play tennis with Uncle Rafa.
M Oh, right.
L Anyway, tell me the rest of your plans.
M Well, tomorrow morning I'm going to go to the beach and in the afternoon I have a ticket for an American football game. But Thursday is the best day. I'm going to spend the day at Disneyland!
L Wow! That sounds fantastic.
M It is – America is great! After Los Angeles, I'm going to take a bus to Las Vegas, and after that, Dallas and New Orleans.
L Well, have a good time.
M Thanks, Lucas. Tell Mum and Dad I'll phone them tomorrow.
L Will do! They'll be happy to hear from you. Bye!
M Bye!

Acknowledgements

The authors and publishers acknowledge the following sources of copyright material and are grateful for the permissions granted. While every effort has been made, it has not always been possible to identify the sources of all the material used, or to trace all copyright holders. If any omissions are brought to our notice, we will be happy to include the appropriate acknowledgements on reprinting and in the next update to the digital edition, as applicable.

Key: U = Unit

Photographs

All the photographs are sourced from Getty Images.
U1: RichVintage/E+; Anastasiia_M/iStock/Getty Images Plus; Clive Brunskill/Getty Images Sport; Patrik Giardino/Stone; Morsa Images/DigitalVision; JohnnyGreig/E+; YurolaitsAlbert/iStock/Getty Images Plus; Visualspace/E+; **U2:** Grace Cary/Moment; Urbancow/iStock/Getty Images Plus; Yacobchuk/iStock/Getty Images Plus; Laflor/E+; MarioGuti/E+; Walter Bibikow/DigitalVision; Westend61; **U3:** PeopleImages/iStock/Getty Images Plus; Radionphoto/iStock/Getty Images Plus; Caiaimage; FangXiaNuo/iStock/Getty Images Plus; Creativeye99/iStock/Getty Images Plus; Hispanolistic/E+; LauriPatterson/E+; **U4:** Andresr/E+; Shapecharge/E+; Monkeybusinessimages/iStock/Getty Images Plus; Jacob Rushing/Image Source; LARISA SHPINEVA/iStock Editorial; **U5:** IPGGutenbergUKLtd/iStock/Getty Images Plus; Andreka/iStock/Getty Images Plus; Monkeybusinessimages/iStock/Getty Images Plus; YinYang/E+; JackF/iStock/Getty Images Plus; Hispanolistic/E+; Awl Images; Eyeem/Getty Images; Miljko/E+; gmsphotography/Moment; Aliraza Khatri's Photography/Moment; Nirian/iStock/Getty Images Plus; Andresr/E+; georgeclerk/E+; CaronB/iStock/Getty Images Plus; Recep-bg/E+; **U6:** Milos Dimic/E+; Walter Lockwood/Photolibrary; Michael Blann/DigitalVision; Mike Powell/Allsport Concepts; Chabruken/Taxi; Mediaphotos/E+; Ftwitty/E+; Cecilie_Arcurs/E+; Maskot; Vladimir Godnik; Pixelfit/E+; PeopleImages/E+; Stockvisual/E+; **U7:** Zoranm/E+; Daniela Duncan/Moment; BrianAJackson/iStock/Getty Images Plus; AdrianHancu/iStock/Getty Images Plus; Neyya/iStock/Getty Images Plus; **U8:** Noam Galai/Noamgalai.com/Moment; Czekma13/iStock/Getty Images Plus; Doble.d/Moment Open; Wundervisuals/E+; SeanPavonePhoto/iStock/Getty Images Plus; Pol Albarrán/Moment; **U9:** Ainsley Duyvestyn-Smith/EyeEm; JKristoffersson/iStock/Getty Images Plus; Grafissimo/E+; Polina Chalaia/EyeEm; Car Culture/Getty Images; georgeclerk/iStock Unreleased; bgwalker/iStock Unreleased; Yuri Zhuck/Moment; tupungato/iStock Editorial; Marcus Lindstrom/iStock/Getty Images Plus; J-wildman/iStock/Getty Images Plus; Alexander Spatari/Moment; Robert Daly/OJO Images; Paula Hible/Photolibrary; Panya Kuanun/EyeEm; DarthArt/iStock Editorial; George Pachantouris/Moment; Thomas Northcut/Photodisc; Patrick Keyser/Moment; Pigphoto/iStock/Getty Images Plus; Czekma13/iStock/Getty Images Plus; Allou/iStock/Getty Images Plus; **U10:** StockstudioX/E+; Westend61; Hill Street Studios/DigitalVision; Hero Images; Image Source/DigitalVision; Pixelfit/E+; FotoTravel/iStock/Getty Images Plus; DaniloAndjus/E+; Paul Bradbury/OJO Images; JohnnyGreig/E+; **U11:** Nick David/Stone; _IB_/iStock/Getty Images Plus; Real444/E+; Fuse/Corbis; Dean Mitchell/E+; Photographer Nick Measures/Moment; Klaus Vedfelt/DigitalVision; Mark Williamson/Photodisc; Skynesher/E+; Vanessa Davies/Dorling Kindersley/Getty Images Plus; Vadimguzhva/iStock/Getty Images Plus; KatarzynaBialasiewicz/iStock/Getty Images Plus; Eric Audras/ONOKY; Angelo D'Amico/iStock/Getty Images Plus; Richcano/iStock/Getty Images Plus; Alvarez/E+; Val Thoermer/EyeEm; **U12:** Holger Leue/The Image Bank Unreleased; Simonkr/E+; Valentyn Semenov/EyeEm; Mikkelwilliam/E+; Nena Diana Klopf/EyeEm.

The following photographs are sourced from other libraries.

U1: Shutterstock/William Perugini; **U5:** Shutterstock/Andrey tiyk; **U6:** Shaun Higson/Lifestyle/Alamy Stock Photo; **U10:** s_oleg/Shutterstock; **U12:** Shutterstock/ESB Professional.

Cover photograph by Brandon Colbert Photography/Moment/Getty Images

U8: Commissioned photography by Gareth Boden.

Illustrations

QBS Learning; Mark Bird; Mark Duffin; Sally Elford; John Goodwin (Eye Candy Illustration); Dusan Lakicevic (Beehive Illustration); Roger Penwill; Gavin Reece (New Division); Martin Sanders (Beehive Illustration); Sean 290 (KJA Artists); David Semple; Marie-Eve Tremblay (Colagene); Andrea Turvey (Eye Candy Illustration); Gary Venn (Lemonade Illustration).

Commissioned Video stills by Rob Maidment and Sharp Focus Productions.

Filming in King's College by kind permission of the Provost and Scholars of King's College, Cambridge.

Audio production by Hart McLeod and by Creative Listening.

Typeset by QBS Learning.

Corpus

Development of this publication has made use of the Cambridge English Corpus (CEC). The CEC is a computer database of contemporary spoken and written English, which currently stands at over one billion words. It includes British English, American English and other varieties of English. It also includes the Cambridge Learner Corpus, developed in collaboration with the University of Cambridge ESOL Examinations. Cambridge University Press has built up the CEC to provide evidence about language use that helps us to produce better language teaching materials.

English Profile

This product is informed by English Vocabulary Profile, built as part of English Profile, a collaborative programme designed to enhance the learning, teaching and assessment of English worldwide. Its main funding partners are Cambridge University Press and Cambridge Assessment English and its aim is to create a 'profile' for English, linked to the Common European Framework of Reference for Languages (CEFR). English Profile outcomes, such as the English Vocabulary Profile, will provide detailed information about the language that learners can be expected to demonstrate at each CEFR level, offering a clear benchmark for learners' proficiency. For more information, please visit www.englishprofile.org.

CALD

The Cambridge Advanced Learner's Dictionary is the world's most widely used dictionary for learners of English. Including all the words and phrases that learners are likely to come across, it also has easy-to-understand definitions and example sentences to show how the word is used in context. The Cambridge Advanced Learner's Dictionary is available online at dictionary.cambridge.org.

CAMBRIDGE
UNIVERSITY PRESS

University Printing House, Cambridge CB2 8BS, United Kingdom

One Liberty Plaza, 20th Floor, New York, NY 10006, USA

477 Williamstown Road, Port Melbourne, VIC 3207, Australia

314–321, 3rd Floor, Plot 3, Splendor Forum, Jasola District Centre, New Delhi – 110025, India

103 Penang Road, #05–06/07, Visioncrest Commercial, Singapore 238467

Cambridge University Press is part of the University of Cambridge.

It furthers the University's mission by disseminating knowledge in the pursuit of education, learning and research at the highest international levels of excellence.

cambridge.org
Information on this title: cambridge.org/9781108961738

First published 2022

20 19 18 17 16 15 14 13 12 11 10 9 8 7 6 5 4 3 2 1

Printed in Great Britain by Ashford Colour Press Ltd.

A catalogue record for this publication is available from the British Library

ISBN 978-1-108-95968-1 Starter Student's Book with eBook
ISBN 978-1-108-96169-1 Starter Student's Book with Digital Pack
ISBN 978-1-108-96172-1 Starter Workbook with Answers
ISBN 978-1-108-96173-8 Starter Workbook without Answers
ISBN 978-1-108-96170-7 Starter Combo A with Digital Pack
ISBN 978-1-108-96171-4 Starter Combo B with Digital Pack
ISBN 978-1-108-96174-5 Starter Teacher's Book with Digital Pack
ISBN 978-1-108-95969-8 Starter Presentation Plus

Additional resources for this publication at cambridge.org/empower